Contents

Childhood
Sexual Abuse,
Sexuality,
Pregnancy and Birthing
A Life History Study

Patrica Smith

PCCS BOOKS

Manchester

First published in 1993 by
Inside Out Books,
Palmerston North,
New Zealand.

This edition published in 1995 by
PCCS BOOKS
Paragon House
48 Seymour Grove
Old Trafford
Manchester
M16 0LN

Childhood Sexual Abuse, Sexuality, Pregnancy and Birthing

ISBN 1 898059 10 1

Cover design and printing by
Printoff Graphic Arts Ltd., Alexander House,
Lomeshaye Road, Nelson, Lancashire.

Acknowledgements and Preface

• I would like to thank Sue Webb for supervising this research. Her trust, flexibility, clarity and support were invaluable.

• My thanks also to Kerry Burgess, Nicky Depree and Dianne Stogre-Power for their assistance, support and encouragement at crucial times in the writing up of this material.

• I would like to thank Gary Hermansson for the opportunity to extend the original research project to this Monograph and for his editorial work.

• Special thanks must be given to 'Margaret' and her family. The courage and trust implicit in her sharing was as generous as her story is inspirational.

• Finally, I wish to thank Jareth, Asher and Layli Smith for their patient support and Philip Smith for his ongoing assistance and encouragement.

Patrica Smith, August 1993

This Monograph is based on a Research Project undertaken by the Author in 1992 towards a Master of Guidance and Counselling degree through Massey University, New Zealand. The content breaks new ground and the study is of importance to women who have experienced childhood sexual abuse and to many people working in the health professions and helping services. The quality of the study was such that it was considered desirable to make it widely available.

We wish to thank the Author for making her study available and the subject of the life history study for allowing her story to be told in this form.

Gary Hermansson & Sue Webb
(Directors/Editors: Inside-Out Books)

All thanks to Inside-Out Books and Patrica Smith for making this book available for publication in the UK.

PCCS Books

Abstract

This research explored connections between childhood sexual abuse and sexuality, pregnancy and birthing in one woman's life. Literature was researched initially in relation to the effects of childhood sexual abuse on later functioning and, in particular, its impact on sexuality. Links from sexuality to pregnancy and birthing were then drawn with a view to examining possible connections between childhood sexual abuse and these later experiences. Life history methodology was employed to explore these dimensions of one woman's experience. The exposition of her life highlighted a number of coping strategies, developed initially in response to sexual abuse in childhood, which played a major role in the survivor's intrapsychic, interpersonal, and social functioning. These strategies also profoundly affected her experiences of sexuality, pregnancy and birthing. The implications of these in relation to the gynaecological, antenatal, perinatal and postnatal care of childhood sexual abuse survivors are highlighted.

Introduction

Childhood sexual abuse has received unprecedented attention and recognition in recent years. The prevalence of this childhood trauma and the extent that it impacts on survivors' lives are still only gradually becoming understood. Research in this area, however, is a burgeoning phenomenon. This research project initially set out to explore the potential relationship between childhood sexual abuse and birthing experience in later life. While many studies have examined the long-term effects of sexual abuse on women's lives, interestingly, the connection between childhood sexual abuse and birthing appears largely to have been overlooked.

Although the literature on childhood sexual abuse encompasses four data bases, initially nothing could be found that discussed any links between childhood sexual abuse and later birthing experience. It seemed logical, however, that these experiences would be inextricably linked. Both are major life experiences for some women and both involve invasion of body boundaries, similar parts of the body and sensations that are in general overwhelming. It seemed to be an area deserving of research.

Because of the limited amount of literature, the study was broadened to include sexual experience. The addition of this dimension offered a possible link between the two other experiences. If the literature explored the effects of childhood sexual abuse on later sexual experience and documented common features between sexuality and birthing, then this would increase the likelihood that connections between childhood sexual abuse and birthing could be established.

Childhood sexual abuse, sexuality and birthing are arguably the most personal areas of a woman's life. The method used to investigate these, therefore, needed to be highly sensitive and non-abusive. Life history incorporates subjective experience as a positive feature and can be both collaborative and empowering. A qualitative method of research, life history involves the parallel process of 'looking at the life of an individual as a unique and personal history' (Novitz, 1982) and also recognizes those elements of universality that make up our common experience. Feminists argue that research can be a process of intervention because it enables people to reflect on and possibly perceive their experience in a different light and this in itself can stimulate change (Middleton, 1988; Oakley, 1981). These possibilities helped justify the potentially gross intrusion into the three extremely personal areas of childhood sexual abuse, sexuality and birthing experience that this research demanded. The features and process of life history method are discussed more fully in Chapter 3.

Margaret's story is presented in Chapter 4 as much as possible in her own words. It is an inspiring story of courage, fortitude and resilience of the human spirit. It stands alone, yet it is one of many.

The final chapters of this study discuss and analyse Margaret's story in the light of the literature. Connections are made between the literature on childhood sexual abuse, sexuality, pregnancy and birthing and various features of Margaret's own experience. A number of possible hypotheses and theoretical understandings are put forward. From these further suggestions are made regarding future research and the medical care and treatment of women, particularly in relation to pregnancy and childbirth.

Notes:

1. Throughout this study, childhood sexual abuse is discussed in relation to female experience and, in particular, one woman's experience. Therefore, feminine possessive adjectives and pronouns have been used.
2. The names used in the Life History are fictitious, to protect the identities of those involved.

1
Review of Literature

Introduction

The purpose of this research was to explore the effects that childhood sexual abuse may have on later life experience, particularly in relation to sexuality, pregnancy and birthing.

In recent years awareness of, and information about, childhood sexual abuse has dramatically increased. Clinical understandings, originally the only source of information, are now increasingly supported by community studies, as research on the psychological aftermath of childhood sexual abuse has continued to evolve.

The impact of childhood sexual abuse on later sexual experience has received less attention. It is only in recent years that studies such as Jehu's (1988) at the University of Manitoba, have described the degree and extent of sexual dysfunction resulting from childhood sexual abuse.

Any links between childhood sexual abuse and pregnancy and birth experiences have hardly been addressed; only two papers could be found and both considered only small samples. An examination of some of the dynamics of pregnancy and giving birth, however, revealed a remarkable similarity to the emotional and physical experiences of childhood sexual abuse. Connections between sexual experience and birthing experience have also been made (Kitzinger, 1983; Newton, 1979). This leads to the conclusion that if childhood sexual abuse can affect later sexual experience (Jehu, 1988; Maltz & Holman, 1987), then it is likely also to influence later birthing experience.

This Chapter investigates the literature in the three areas - childhood sexual abuse, sexuality and birthing. After defining and describing the traumatic experience of childhood sexual abuse and the impact this may have in childhood and in adult life, the possible effects of this experience on the emergence and functioning of sexuality are discussed. This is followed by a comparison of sexual experience and birthing experience. The nature and subjective experience for women of pregnancy and birthing are presented, with discussion of the impact of medical procedures on the birthing experience. The roles that anxiety, alienation and somatization, all documented long-term effects of childhood sexual abuse, play in the birth process is given particular attention.

Childhood Sexual Abuse

This section provides a background to the experience of childhood sexual abuse which will lead to a full discussion of its effects. The terminology is defined and initial accommodations are described. Factors affecting prognosis are then discussed.

A Definition of Childhood Sexual Abuse

A widely used definition describes child sexual abuse as the involvement of dependent, developmentally immature children and adolescents in sexual activities that they do not fully comprehend, are unable to give informed consent to, and that violate the social taboos of family roles (Schechter & Roberge, 1976).

The term child sexual abuse then can cover acts ranging from fondling to intercourse, a single assault by a stranger to frequent acts over years by a family member or family friend. Because no standard definition of childhood sexual abuse exists (Mrazek & Mrazek, 1981), key concepts are used in conflicting ways throughout the literature. Childhood sexual abuse is, for example, distinguished from incest by some writers and not by others.

Courtois (1991) wrote that incest is the most prevalent form of child sexual abuse and the one most damaging to the child. She used the comprehensive definition of Schechter and Roberge (1976) which described incest as sexual contact with a person who would be considered an ineligible partner because of his blood and/or social ties (i.e. kin) to the subject and her family (p.32).

This term, therefore, includes several categories of partners, including father, stepfather, etc. It also includes what is named 'quasi-family'; that is, parental and family friends, because the incest taboo applies in a weakened form to all those people from whom "the female child should rightfully expect warmth or protection and sexual distance".

Similarly, Ellenson's (1986) definition, cited in Frawley and McInerney (1987), described incest as repeated physical contact of a sexual nature between an adult who has violated a position of trust or authority or caretaking role (regardless of kinship) and a child (p.150).

The significance lies in the abuse of trust and authority and the ongoing nature of the abuse. The majority of adults who sexually abuse children occupy a kinship or trusted relationship (Summit, 1983). The presence of a relationship between perpetrator and victim adds to the traumatic impact of the abuse and introduces features such as the adult's access to the child because of kinship and authority, secrecy, betrayal of trust, the child's powerlessness and the repeated nature of the abuse (Courtois, 1988).

Child sexual abuse is therefore complex, and covers a wide range of behaviour between individuals of varying degrees of relatedness. It involves one or multiple acts of sexual violation over time, ranging from months to years, generally in an escalating pattern. Force or some form of coercion is inevitable and can be subtle, especially at the beginning, generally happening under the guise of affection. Children often appear to submit passively to involved adults' wishes, possibly in return for affection, favours and/or material gifts (Courtois, 1988). That the child is unable to give informed consent is implicit in the definition given and this underlines the power imbalance that lies at the heart of this issue, highlighting as it does the child's helplessness (Summit, 1983).

The Initial Accommodation to Childhood Sexual Abuse

It is difficult to understand the dynamics that operate in child sexual abuse and serve to maintain the gross intrusion that it constitutes, keeping child victims virtual hostages in their own lives.

Summit (1983) offered an excellent explanation derived from many sexual abuse treatment centres and thousands of reports and complaints. He defined a 'child abuse accommodation syndrome' made up of five categories of which two, 'secrecy' and 'helplessness', are necessary conditions within which sexual abuse occurs. The other three, 'entrapment and accommodation', 'delayed and conflicted disclosure', and 'retraction' may follow on sequentially with increasing complexity and variability. Summit wrote that each category 'reflects a compelling reality for the victim'. (1983, p.181)

Secrecy was his first category. The child is totally dependent on the perpetrator's assignation of reality to the experience and the requirement of secrecy is inevitable. The secrecy conveys to the child the danger and menace - it promises safety and conveys fear. Attempts to tell meet with adult disbelief and silence and Summit emphasized that while most people assume a victim would seek help, the majority of victims tell no one.

Helplessness, the second prerequisite for child sexual abuse, he defined as arising in part from secrecy. Children are rendered helpless by society's expectation that they be obedient and affectionate to any adult entrusted with their care. Children are three times more likely to be abused by a known adult than a stranger (Finkelhor, 1986; Summit 1983). Summit (1983) emphasized the point that because loss of love or loss of family security is the most terrifying scenario for a child, dependent children are generally helpless to resist or complain.

Entrapment and accommodation, Summit's third category, are then inevitable for the sexually abused child, because the adaptive healthy response is to accept the situation and survive. The means by which a child accommodates sexual abuse vary, but ultimately require the child, in order to achieve some sense of power and control in the face of overwhelming intrusion, to assume some responsibility and attempt to be 'good', for which there is an implicit or explicit promise of reward by the perpetrator. The child then may have both the power to destroy the family and the responsibility to keep it together. Normal values are upturned - lying and maintaining the secret is 'right', telling the secret is wrong. In order to survive the child establishes various accommodation mechanisms; for example delinquent behaviour, self-destructiveness, altered states of consciousness or splitting off reality.

While most ongoing sexual abuse is never disclosed, the child who attempts to do so usually faces a disbelieving audience. Children often accommodate the abuse by hiding any conflict and trying especially hard to please. Whether the child is acting out and compulsively sexual or seemingly well-adjusted, such behaviour will generally be interpreted to invalidate her complaint. If the child does disclose, the likelihood is she will retract or change the story, as the fears and threats on which the secrecy depended are seen as likely to come true (Summit, 1983). '

Without any permission or power to disclose what is happening to them, and in the face of adults' generally disbelieving and punitive responses, sexually abused children typically condemn themselves to a life without intimacy, trust or self-validation.

Contributing Factors Affecting Prognosis

Important variables that influence and mediate after-effects, immediate and long-term, include the extent of sexual contact, age of onset, degree of relatedness and age difference between victim and perpetrator and length of contact. Other issues that need consideration are the presence of pathology or dysfunction in the family prior to the abuse, for example marital problems, neglect, deprivation, violence, and factors such as the individual child's cognitive capacity, temperament and health (Courtois, 1988; Sheldrick, 1991).

Browne and Finkelhor (1986), while acknowledging a lack of agreement in the literature about what factors affect prognosis, stated that there are trends in the findings. They noted four factors that indicate increased negative impact: (i) abuse by fathers or stepfathers, (ii) experiences involving genital abuse, (iii) the presence of force, and, (iv) where the abusers are adult men.

They also noted that the relationship between the age of onset and the extent of trauma was a complex issue that had been insufficiently studied. While some studies suggested that younger children were more vulnerable to trauma, others found no such relationship.

One of the major difficulties associated with such research is the issue of repression. There is some evidence (Courtois, 1988; Herman & Schatzow, 1987), suggesting that young children use massive repression as their primary cgo defence mechanism and as the abuse is 'forgotten', it is unreported and unacknowledged. Additionally, increased memory loss has been associated with a greater experience of sadistic or violent abuse (Courtois, 1991).

Lundberg-Love, Marmion, Ford, Geffner and Peacock (1991), in commenting that incest survivors reported both more and higher levels of psychological symptoms than non-abused women seeking therapy, noted that most survivors sought treatment for reasons other than recovery. The authors stated that in their experience between 25-50% of survivors had no recollection of their abuse when they entered treatment. Similarly, Courtois (1991) noted new data which suggested that amnesia was the most common feature of childhood sexual abuse and that possibly half of all survivors did not remember the abuse.

The consequences of this in relation to both empirical studies and mental health and medical treatment for women are extensive. Perhaps it is one of the factors contributing to the differing results in many empirical studies, as stated by Browne and Finkelhor (1986). Comparison groups of non-abused women may in fact contain survivors who have no memory of having been abused.

This section has provided a working definition of childhood sexual abuse and outlined some of its features. It has described how children manage to accommodate this trauma in their lives and presented the factors that effect long-term prognosis. The following section will examine the effects of childhood sexual abuse. It considers the impact in terms of Post-traumatic Stress Syndrome and discusses the emotional and physical experience and the interpersonal, social and sexual functioning of survivors.

The Effects of Childhood Sexual Abuse

Currently there is little agreement about the short-term or long-term effects of child sexual abuse (Sheldrick, 1991). While a few studies have reported that the experience may contribute positively to development (Brunngraber, 1986; Kinsey, Pomeroy, Martin & Gebhard, 1953), most have reported adverse long- and short-term effects.

The two main sources of information about the effects of child sexual abuse are (i) self reports of and clinical reports on survivors, and, (ii) an increasing number of empirical studies. The latter are relatively new and many have methodological problems, such as biased or small samples, absence of control groups and inadequate or subjective outcome measures, which render their findings less reliable (Briere & Runtz, 1989; Browne & Finkelhor, 1986; Sheldrick, 1991).

Browne and Finkelhor (1986), however, concluded, in their review of empirical studies of after-effects of sexual abuse, that between one- and two-fifths of sexually abused children showed pathological disturbance immediately after the abuse. As adults, survivors as a group showed impairment compared with non-abused adults and, of these, one-fifth had serious psychopathology. An important consideration raised by Browne and Finkelhor (1986) was that effects may be age and phase specific, so that effects seen in children may not persist into adulthood. It is also important to note that the range of responses is wide and they vary enormously. For example, children's learning may be seriously impaired or, conversely, they may excel. Similarly, in adolescence, rage may be acted out in rebellious delinquent behaviour or may be suppressed in depression or compliant 'good girl' behaviour.

The long-term effects of childhood sexual abuse are defined by Browne and Finkelhor (1986) as those which develop two years or more after the abuse. Although many empirical studies suffer from the faults outlined earlier, they do support clinical reports that child sexual abuse is related to psychological, sexual and social dysfunctioning in adulthood. Symptoms include depression, negative self-esteem, self-destructiveness, interpersonal problems, sexual problems and a tendency to revictimization and substance abuse (Bergart, 1986; Blake-White & Kline, 1985; Briere & Runtz, 1989; Browne & Finkelhor, 1986; Peters, 1988).

Lundberg-Love, et al. (1991), in a well designed study that systematically assessed the long-term consequences of childhood sexual abuse, used a number of standard psychological measures and compared the results with female control groups without any history of childhood sexual abuse. They concluded that the long-term consequences were many and varied. They described survivors as having higher levels of psychological distress, more types of symptomatology and as being significantly more depressed, alienated, inhibited and socially introverted. However, in relation to interpersonal functioning, childhood sexual abuse survivors were more sensitive to others than the three control groups used.

In relation to women's mental health treatment, Mullen, Romans-Clarkson, Walton and Herbison (1988) noted the over-representation of women among people with depressive and anxiety disorders and suggested that psychiatric researchers have to date ignored the effect childhood sexual abuse has had on women's lives. The findings of a community study of three thousand randomly selected people, conducted by Stein, Golding, Siegal, Burnam and Sorenson (1989), highlighted the pervasiveness of psychological symptoms and psychiatric diagnosis in the years after childhood sexual abuse. Lundberg-Love, et al. (1991) found that the MMPI was useful in differentiating between survivors and non-survivors and suggested that the inventory might have some potential as a screening device to identify women who are survivors.

Post-traumatic Stress Disorder

Childhood sexual abuse survivors often experience Post-traumatic Stress Disorder (Blake-White & Kline, 1985; Cole & Barney, 1987; Courtois, 1991). This is usually untreated and may naturally go away in time, or lie dormant for years before coming out as a result of life experiences and triggers, or it can effect the survivor continuously throughout her life without her being aware of it (Courtois, 1991). Memory deficits, amnesia and dissociation are characteristic responses to trauma, and, along with other ways of coping like minimalizing, denial and rationalization, need to be seen as adaptive responses or functional and understandable reactions to childhood sexual abuse.

The symptoms of Post-traumatic Stress Disorder occur in two major phases; phases of denial and phases of a more intrusive nature, with survivors swinging between these. Symptoms associated with the numbing or denial phase include repression, dissociation, partial or complete amnesia, forgetfulness, minimizing, fatigue, headaches and selective inattention. Intrusive/ reliving phase symptoms include hyper-activity and hyper-vigilance, startle responses, repeated thoughts and imagery in the form of flashbacks, confusion, waves of intense emotions and nightmares (Cole & Barney, 1987; Courtois, 1991). Both sets of symptoms cause discomfort and may lead survivors to seek treatment.

Clinicians have in the past been reluctant to work with traumatic memories and the strong affect that can accompany them. More recently, the importance of focusing on integrating the content and affect of the trauma into a logical experience of personal history and sense of self has been demonstrated (Cornell & Olio, 1991; Courtois, 1988). Herman and Schatzow (1987) wrote:

> *'. . . the retrieval and validation of repressed memories has an important role in the recovery process. With the return of the memory, the patient has an opportunity as an adult to integrate an experience that was beyond her capacity to endure as a child. The purpose of reliving the experience with full affect is not simply one of the catharsis, but of reintegration.'* (p.12)

Denial and dissociation are the two most common functional responses to bodily trauma (Cornell & Olio, 1991; Courtois, 1991). In dissociative states the mind, rather than integrating elements of consciousness, affect, identity and behaviour, splits them off, thereby disintegrating rather than integrating experience. This results in a... diminished capacity for spontaneous affect, often a fragmented sense of identity, and ultimately a loss of personal history (Cornell & Olio, 1991, p. 61). While it can manifest as a major break in consciousness, more often it is a subtle and persistent break in consciousness or in contact with others.

Denial is a primitive and unconscious way of dealing with intolerable conflict, anxiety or pain and is used to maintain survival. Cornell and Olio (1991) stated that in adult survivors denial ranges from denial of the abuse experience to denial of its importance and effects. Courtois (1988) also identified denial patterns as originating in the family, which characteristically use it to cope with difficult issues. Cornell and Olio (1991) suggested that used together each of these two defences becomes more entrenched, so that they form a more cohesive coping strategy than either used alone. They described this experience as becoming 'numb and dumb' and surmised that 'it is easier to deny the existence or significance of an experience one does not feel'. (p.61)

A number of events are known to act as triggers to memory retrieval in survivors. Courtois (1991) has organized these into five categories:

1. Normal developmental events or crises, like birth and death.
2. Exposure to events that are like the original trauma.
3. Crises that directly concern the survivor's trauma, e.g. disclosure.
4. Issues that arise in therapy
5. Life stages such as mid-life crisis.

Courtois (1991) stated that memory retrieval can occur in different ways and usually happens in a disconnected and fragmented way. Body memories and perceptions like colours, images, sounds, smells, and tastes can prompt recall. The body might react by producing pain that resembles the pain of the abuse and physical stigmata can occur as the memory of the abuse is recalled. Similarly, memories can show somatically in the form of illness, pain or conversion symptoms such as paralysis and numbing. Memories can also return emotionally, with the survivor experiencing sudden, intense feelings or more subtle shifts in mood. Flashbacks and nightmares are other common disturbing experiences (Courtois, 1991). These memories provide disparate and fragmented evidence of the original abuse. Courtois (1991), in connection with the process, used the meaningful image of the survivor piecing together a giant jigsaw as she tries to recover her personal history and identity.

Emotional Reactions and Self-Perceptions

The most commonly cited symptom for adult survivors is depression (Browne & Finkelhor, 1986). The sense of betrayal, powerlessness and stigmatization felt by survivors is often experienced as underlying rage, which is generally directed towards the self in self-destructive behaviour, suicidal thoughts and attempts (Briere & Runtz, 1989; Browne & Finkelhor,

1986; Courtois, 1988). The pervading sense of powerlessness survivors experience may also contribute to their reported high levels of generalized anxiety and fear, which is expressed through tension, phobias and sleep disturbances (Briere & Runtz, 1989; Browne & Finkelhor, 1986; Courtois, 1988; Sheldrick, 1991).

Feelings of low self-esteem and inadequacy are particularly common among sexual abuse survivors (Bachmann, Moeller & Benett, 1988; Briere & Runtz, 1989; Browne & Finkelhor, 1986; Courtois, 1988; Jehu, Gazan & Klassen, 1985). This reflects the deep seated shame and guilt many survivors have reported (Bergart, 1986; Deighton & McPeek, 1985; Frawley & McInerney, 1987; Gordy, 1983) and the feelings of responsibility and self blame they often take on themselves for the abuse occurring (Courtois, 1988; Knight, 1990).

Physical and Somatic Effects

Courtois (1988) discussed physical and somatic effects in relation to negative self feelings. Many survivors extended their self hatred to their bodies (Courtois, 1988; Frawley & McInerney, 1987), maintaining behaviour patterns learned during the abuse. These enabled them to disregard bodily needs so that they did not experience impulses to eat, rest or sleep (Courtois, 1988). Bachmann, et al. (1988) listed a variety of somatic dysfunctions commonly reported by sexual abuse survivors, including sleep disorders, tension, abdominal distress, headaches, backaches and complaints of chronic pain with no identifiable physical causes.

A number of studies reported an association between pelvic pain and other gynaecological complaints and child sexual abuse (Bachmann, et al., 1988; Harrop-Griffeths, Katon, Walker, Holm, Russo & Hickok, 1988). Paddison, Gise, Lebovits, Strain, Cirasole and Levine (1990) reported a connection between sexual abuse and psychiatric hospitalization for women seeking help for Premenstrual Syndrome. Harrop-Griffeths, et al. (1988), in a small study involving twenty five patients with chronic pelvic pain and a control group of thirty with specific gynaecological problems, showed a significantly higher occurrence of major depression, substance abuse, adult sexual dysfunction, somatization and a history of child and adult sexual abuse in those with pelvic pain. They concluded that chronic pelvic pain may cover chronic psychological pain, acting as a coping mechanism to protect against painful memories.

Courtois (1988) also reported survivors experiencing marked difficulty undergoing any type of medical procedure, particularly those that are surgical or gynaecological in nature. Medical people were often feared because they are authority figures with power and control (Bachmann, et al., 1988) and also because their methods are usually invasive, focusing on one aspect of the body - not the whole person (Courtois, 1988). Courtois identified a variety of coping methods sexual abuse survivors used to deal with medical personnel. Avoidance was common, especially if dissociation and denial were primary coping strategies for the survivor, as was over-compliance and a reluctance to 'bother the doctor'.

Courtois (1988) also noted that physical examinations which used touch, especially examinations of breasts, pelvic or rectal areas, were very disturbing for survivors, as were procedures like catheterization, intravenous treatment and surgery. For a sexually abused woman, to have her body exposed, or be kept waiting due to delays or administrative procedures, can invoke fear and panic as this risks replicating aspects of the original experience, triggering flashbacks, dissociation or stimulating body memories.

Oppenheimer, Howells and Palmer (1985) reported a link between child sexual abuse and eating disorders. This was also found by Lobel (1991) in her study which explored and confirmed a relationship between childhood sexual abuse and borderline personality disorder. In a patient sample Morrison (1989) found increased likelihood of somatization disorder in those suffering sexual abuse as children compared to a control group, and Briere and Runtz (1988) demonstrated a link between dissociation and somatization in students who had been abused as children.

Effects on Interpersonal Relating

Sexual abuse survivors often have problems in their interpersonal relationships. An inability to trust due to underlying feelings of fear, hostility and a sense of betrayal has been widely reported (Browne & Finkelhor, 1986; Courtois, 1988; Jehu, 1988; Sheldrick, 1991). Survivors therefore have particular difficulty with intimate relationships (Browne & Finkelhor, 1986; Courtois, 1988; Gordy, 1983) and are often unable to allow closeness beyond a certain point.

Most survivors experience a deep sense of loneliness (Bergart, 1986). Many suffer from severe feelings of isolation and alienation (Bergart, 1986; Blake-White & Kline, 1985; Browne & Finkelhor, 1986; Gordy, 1983; Sheldrick, 1991) as the secrecy of their abuse experience creates barriers and hides the innate sense of badness and being different many feel (Bergart, 1986; Knight, 1990).

Similarly, a sexual abuse survivor's need for control in interpersonal relationships might become the main feature of her social functioning as she struggles to overcome feelings of powerlessness (Bachmann, et al., 1988). Conversely, the survivor, acting from these feelings of powerlessness, may feel she has no control in her interpersonal relationships and does not deserve any because of her essential worthlessness (Knight,

1990). The survivor, then, is at risk of being further victimized sexually, emotionally and/or physically.

Sexual revictimization as adults, both inside and outside the family, has been another commonly reported occurrence, as is the increased likelihood that adult sexual abuse survivors will have physically violent and/or sexually assaulting husbands (Browne & Finkelhor, 1986; Courtois, 1988; Frawley & McInerney, 1987; Jehu, 1988; Russell, 1986).

Difficulties with relationships due to past abuse also mean survivors have increased likelihood of parenting difficulties with their own children. Often a poor relationship pattern with parents gets repeated and unresolved issues around abuse mean that survivors maintain emotional and physical distance with their own children, possibly even leading to abuse (Browne & Finkelhor, 1986; Courtois, 1988; Sheldrick, 1991). Conversely, some survivors are outstanding parents, determined to give their children more than they received (Courtois, 1988; Gordy, 1983).

Effects on Social Functioning

Courtois (1988) reported wide variability in the social functioning of survivors, ranging from over functioning and compulsive social interaction to isolation and antisocial behaviour. Several studies of specific populations have shown that childhood sexual abuse was definitely a factor in the development of antisocial and deviant behaviour such as prostitution, alcohol abuse and drug abuse (Bergart, 1986; Browne & Finkelhor, 1986; Courtois, 1991; Sheldrick, 1991).

The effects of childhood sexual abuse on career development and occupational functioning needs further exploration (Courtois, 1988). Sheldrick (1991) noted that survivors may experience educational difficulties that affect later career choice and Lobel (1991) found that those women sexually abused as children had, on average, two years less formal education than those not abused.

Brunngraber (1986) cited positive outcomes in her study of college students where survivors of child sexual abuse had learned important attributes of self reliance, autonomy, independence, accountability and sensitivity towards others. She postulated these qualities represent mechanisms developed to cope with the abuse. Similarly, some survivors have been able to extend a childhood pattern of successful school functioning to social, career and family arenas (Courtois, 1988; Gordy, 1983). Courtois (1988) noted skills learned in childhood, such as perceptiveness about others' needs, compliant behaviour especially to authority figures, meeting others' needs and a capacity to handle multiple stresses and responsibilities, contributed to the success of many abused individuals.

However, she wrote that despite apparent success many of these women described themselves feeling unconnected to their accomplishments and saw themselves as 'imposters waiting to be found out'. (p.114) This lack of pleasure and satisfaction in accomplishment reflected the degree to which life experience had become separated from the self and emotional experience (Cornell & Olio, 1991). Moreover, Herman and Schatzow (1987), commenting on a similar pattern, described a marked contrast between the success in these women's working lives and the constriction and isolation in their intimate relationships. Further, they considered that, while many survivors managed to meet others' needs effectively, they were often very poor at caring for themselves.

Effects on Sexual Functioning

Childhood sexual abuse violates important physical and emotional boundaries. It is a gross betrayal of trust and an abuse of power. Because it occurs at a sexual level, childhood sexual abuse can influence adult survivors' enjoyment of sexual contact and interfere with the expression of their sexuality.

Results of clinical and community studies have shown later problems in sexual functioning and in adjustment of childhood sexual abuse survivors (Bergart, 1986; Browne & Finkelhor, 1986; Courtois, 1988; Sheldrick, 1991). Jehu's (1988) work with a large clinical sample showed a prevalence of some sexual dysfunction in 94% of women sexually abused as children. Survivors were likely to have lower levels of sexual self-esteem (Sheldrick, 1991) and experienced basic struggles with sexual compatibility, finding it difficult often to combine sex and affection with the same man (Gordy, 1983).

Maltz and Holman (1987) outlined three major areas where childhood sexual abuse affected later sexual behaviour. Two of these areas, 'sexual emergence in adolescence' and 'sexual arousal, response and preference', are relevant to the current study. While acknowledging childhood sexual abuse as a major influence in sexual development and expression, Maltz and Holman stressed that other factors also play important roles. Such elements as biological drive, religious beliefs, educational understanding and social group, need to be considered and the extent of their influence deserved further research.

Survivors moving into early adulthood typically develop one of two sexual styles - either social or sexual withdrawal or indiscriminate sexual activity. Some survivors swing between the two (Courtois, 1988; Maltz & Holman, 1987; Sheldrick, 1991). Courtois postulated that the withdrawal and celibacy option reflected fears, negative self feelings and avoidance of sexual identity. Frequent sexual activity might be self-destructive, could result in revictimization or could be an attempt at reclaiming power.

Symptoms of the withdrawal option include refusing dates, staying socially isolated, pretending that sex does not exist and denying sexual feelings (Maltz & Holman, 1987). Many survivors have distorted ideas of what was expected of them and think sexual activity is a necessary part of dating. Some also have no confidence in their ability to say 'No,' and use avoidance in order not to feel overwhelmed and powerless.

The most common sexual dysfunctions reported by childhood sexual abuse survivors have included sexual phobia/aversion, sexual dissatisfaction, impaired sexual motivation arousal and orgasm, dyspareunia (painful sexual intercourse) and vaginismus (vaginal muscle spasms) (Deighton & McPeek, 1985; Jehu, 1988). McGuire and Wagner (1978), from their clinical work, reported that dysfunction around arousal - lack of initiating, lack of sexual appetite and difficulties with sensuality - were common but survivors were often orgasmic, though generally only through intercourse. Often sexual dysfunctions were not manifested immediately and only became apparent when a relationship became closer and more established (Brunngraber, 1986; Jehu, 1988; Sheldrick, 1991).

Factors also perceived as impairing sexual functioning included post-traumatic stress reactions and negative conditioning. These included flashbacks or memories triggered by sexual behaviours, positions, feelings, sounds and smells, or symptoms such as depersonalization, derealization and dissociation which enable the survivor to be sexual without being present (Deighton & McPeek, 1985; Gordy, 1983; Bergart, 1986). Other indications noted earlier such as hyper-alertness, the inability to relax and avoiding situations that trigger traumatic memories or symptoms, also interfere with sexual functioning (Courtois, 1988; Sheldrick, 1991; Bergart, 1986). Flashbacks may cause a recurrence of physical sensations like pain and nausea or can cause a physiological response, such as the tightening of certain muscle groups which work against the arousal process.

The impact of childhood sexual abuse on many survivors lives is deep and enduring. While some effects may be positive most are detrimental. Survivors may experience Post-traumatic Stress Disorder and commonly develop denial and dissociation strategies to handle this. The abuse affects how they see themselves, how they feel at an emotional and physical level, their capacity to interact with others and the effectiveness of their social functioning. In the area of sexual functioning in particular effects are often blatant and intrusive.

Sexuality, Pregnancy, Birthing and Childhood Sexual Abuse

Sexual development, arousal, response and performance are all affected by childhood sexual abuse. While some survivors may be aware of this, the links between their sexuality and their experience of pregnancy and giving birth are unlikely to be made. This is partly because the connection between sexuality and birthing is generally unacknowledged. Pregnancy and birth need to be viewed not as medical conditions, but as part of a woman's psychosexual experience. Where sexuality is more openly dealt with women give birth more easily (Leifer, 1980). Kitzinger (1983) and Newton (1979) both emphasized the importance of regarding sex, birthing and motherhood as part of an inter-related continuum, rather than as different and conflicting experiences.

Linking Sexuality, Pregnancy and Birthing

The connection between birthing and sexuality, though well documented, is largely ignored in our society. There are a number of reasons for this. The emphasis has tended to fall on those aspects of female sexuality that are specifically related to adult men. As a result, women's responses during intercourse have been well documented but other aspects of their sexuality have been largely ignored (Newton, 1973). Also, many of the medical procedures prevalent in our culture have made it difficult for women to discover anything sexual in labour (Kitzinger, 1983). Similarly, current social taboos have effectively inhibited the acknowledgment of sexuality as part of labour or breastfeeding (Newton, 1979).

In western culture, where women have been portrayed as sexual objects advertising anything from paint to freight haulage, the female body is slim and shapely. Pregnant women's bodies are therefore desexualized (Young, 1984). A number of studies (Langer, Taylor, Fiske & Chanowitz, 1976; Taylor & Langer, 1977 cited in Leifer, 1980) found that pregnant women were socially stigmatized, being both stared at and avoided in the same manner as disabled people. While the lack of sexual expectation may be a relief for a survivor experiencing conflicts around sex, the social responses noted may be more disturbing for survivors if they already have low self-esteem and a negative self image.

A woman's body image and her fantasies about her body subtly affect her sexual feelings (Kitzinger, 1983). The negative messages from society and the general view that pregnancy is a medical condition, probably make it difficult for any pregnant woman to experience herself sexually. Women who were sexually abused as children, through low sexual self-esteem and negative self feelings risk being doubly disadvantaged therefore.

Kitzinger also emphasized the importance of having a loving sexual relationship during pregnancy, not only because sexual pleasure is nurturing but also because sexual arousal releases oxytocin into the blood stream. This hormone, which tones the uterus, accumulates in the last few weeks of pregnancy and leads to the spontaneous start of labour. As childhood sexual abuse survivors generally experience a high rate of sexual dysfunction, it is likely that their sexual response is more impaired than other women's during pregnancy and their production of oxytocin may be more limited.

The relationship between natural childbirth and sexual feelings has been well established (Boadella, 1987; Kitzinger, 1983; Newton, 1979). Newton (1979) believed that to understand female sexuality fully all a woman's reproductive behaviours needed to be considered. She suggested that women have three interpersonal acts of reproductive behaviour - intercourse, birthing and breastfeeding - and wrote that a woman's psychological and physiological responses to all three are similar.

Newton (1979) and Kitzinger (1983) both described a number of characteristics that uninhibited, undrugged labour and sexual excitement have in common. These are: breathing pattern, vocalization, facial expression, uterine reactions, cervical reactions, abdominal muscle reactions, central nervous system reactions, strength and flexibility, sensory perception and emotional response. Kitzinger (1983), writing on the intense sexuality of natural birth, stated that it

> *'. . . can be the most intensely sexual experience a woman ever experiences, as strong as orgasm, even more compelling than orgasm. Some women find it disturbing because it is sexual and they feel out of controls as the energy floods through them and they can do nothing to prevent it.'* (p. 210)

This noted similarity between birthing and sexuality risks severely impacting on a sexual abuse survivor. Because of the conflict a survivor may already experience around sexuality, the lack of control and intense sexual feelings described above are unlikely to be experienced as pleasurable and the survivor may need to defend strongly against this. Her previous ways of coping may need to be called on and it is likely that these would then interfere with the natural progression of labour.

Newton (1979) also described certain psychophysiologic similarities between breastfeeding and sexual intercourse and suggested that an accepting attitude towards sexuality may be related to an accepting attitude towards breastfeeding. She acknowledged, however, that current social patterns are very effective in inhibiting this.

Sexuality, birthing and breast feeding are all part of women's psychosexual experience, eliciting similar psychological and physiological responses. There is a likelihood, therefore, that childhood sexual abuse will negatively impact on birthing and breast feeding, given its negative effects on sexuality. There are many factors that combine to make pregnancy and birthing in Western society a conflicted and difficult experience for women. These will be outlined in the following section, with particular attention given to those factors that may make this experience even more difficult for sexual abuse survivors.

Pregnancy and Childbirth as a Transitional Crisis

Pregnancy and childbirth together form a major life event; an important physical and psychological rite of passage in a woman's life. They involve profound psychological and physical changes. Having a child, especially a first child, requires changes in a woman's interpersonal relationships and the dynamics of her family. It creates dramatic changes in her body and appearance, in her physiology and in her social status.

Pregnancy and birthing are recognized in the psychological literature as a 'normal developmental' or 'transitional crisis' (Benedek, 1970; Blum, 1980; Raphael-Leff, 1980). Because personality is not fixed at adolescence but continues to change through the life cycle, these transitional crises provide the potential for a new stage of personality change, reorganization and integration (Grossman, Eichler, & Winickoff, 1980). As with other life transitions, pregnancy and childbirth arouse feelings about adequacy, fears and hopes for the future and memories of relationships to past generations (Blum, 1980).

While most women negotiate the developmental tasks of pregnancy and childbirth, there are some for whom this is particularly difficult. These are the women, who, on top of the normal demands of pregnancy, have to contend with other life events. Raphael-Leff (1980, p.177) described these at risk women as undergoing 'double crisis' adjustment. Included in this category were women who had suffered unforeseen and sudden life events like bereavement and moving, or those who had to contend with ongoing and chronic life events such as adolescence or menopause, diabetes, serious illness, or eating disorders. For a number of reasons, women who were sexually abused as children may also fall into this category.

Psychological Tasks of Pregnancy and Childhood Sexual Abuse

While modern science has in some respects improved the level of physical safety for mother and baby, the pregnant woman's psychological and emotional safety has been largely ignored (Raphael-Leff, 1980). Very few psychological studies have attempted to understand women's subjective experience of pregnancy. Most have examined adjustment to pregnancy, with a view to hypothesizing links to postpartum adjustment. The importance of pregnancy itself for women has been largely ignored (Leifer, 1980).

Pregnancy, especially first pregnancy, necessitates a reappraisal and redefinition of identity. A time of psychological upheaval, it causes changes in a woman's sense of self and in her relationships to significant others, and it also tests her capacity for intimacy and attachment (Offerman-Zuckerberg, 1980). As previously discussed, a woman who has been sexually abused in childhood may already be struggling with some or all of these areas in her life.

Pregnancy is a time of increased attention to the self (Offerman-Zuckerberg, 1980). Psychoanalytic theorists see the fundamental psychological tasks of pregnancy as, initially, attachment to the foetus and, later, differentiation and separation from it (Offerman-Zuckerberg, 1980; Raphael-Leff, 1980; Turrini, 1980). The mother then has first to accept and incorporate the foetus. Many women, according to Offerman-Zuckerberg (1980), have difficulty with the idea of something "other" growing inside them that is beyond their control, and equally difficult can be the adjustment to sharing her body with someone else (Raphael-Leff, 1980). Both of these requirements may present a source of conflict for sexual abuse survivors.

Once the baby has 'moved' it needs to be recognized as a separate entity. Psychological preparation for delivery is complete when the reality of the coming baby is accepted and the mother feels an attachment to it yet separate from it. Thus attachment and separation are crucial issues that go on throughout pregnancy (Offerman-Zuckerberg, 1980) and the pregnant woman is constantly re-negotiating issues around separateness, autonomy and dependency, all of these relevant to the functioning of women who were sexually abused as children.

A profound change required of the pregnant woman, then, is adjustment to a rapidly changing self-concept (Raphael-Leff, 1980). She can no longer consider herself as an independent unit, as she is irreversibly in a mother-child relationship. She is needing to clarify her sense of self in her caretaking role, in her relationship to her partner, to a prospective dependent child and to her own parents (Offerman-Zuckerberg, 1980).

Not only is her sense of self being challenged, her body image is rapidly changing. Raphael-Leff (1980, p.182) described the need for the pregnant woman to expand her consciousness in order to include her previously 'dormant and unexplored womb'.

Similarly, she has to adjust to tender and expanding breasts and a rapidly expanding body. The pregnant woman then is 'thrown onto awareness' of her body, becoming aware of herself as a body (Young, 1984). While Young suggested that pregnant women experience this positively, it may not be so for sexually abused women who, as previously discussed, can feel considerable hatred and denial of bodily experience and sensations.

Young (1984) elaborated further on the phenomenon of the 'unity of self' dissolving over pregnancy and suggested that the experience reveals in several ways a body subjectivity that is de-centred, split or doubled. Pregnant women, she postulated, experience their bodies as having fluid boundaries without a firm sense of where their body ends and the world begins. The pregnant woman experiences her body as another's space and at the same time her own. This blurring of body boundaries could present a problem to a woman who has trouble establishing and maintaining boundaries under normal circumstances.

Pregnancy is also a 'visible manifestation to the outside world' of having had a sexual relationship (Raphael-Leff 1980, p.183). For women who experience conflict around sexuality, it is possible that this could be disturbing. Equally disturbing could be the revival of 'childhood envies and jealousies, shame and guilt' commonly described in the psychoanalytic literature (Raphael-Leff, 1980; Turrini, 1980).

Romanik (1982) described five cases in which incest survivors developed, during pregnancy, symptoms that could be related to their childhood trauma. The women in his sample had received no therapy, nor told anyone of their childhood experience. Their predominant response to pregnancy was denial and rejection. All five women remembered fearing pregnancy during their childhood abuse experience and also feared that their children would also experience sexual victimization. For these women, pregnancy seemed to revive specific unresolved conflicts arising from their experience of incest. While the sample was small and cannot be generalized from, it does suggest that pregnancy may present specific stresses for survivors of childhood sexual abuse.

The profound emotional disequilibrium and emotional lability of the pregnant woman has been stressed by some authors (Offerman-Zuckerberg, 1980; Raphael-Leff, 1980). Bibring (1959, cited in Turrini, 1980) noted severe psychological disturbances in pregnant women who had previously been without symptoms or psychopathology. Raphael-Leff (1980) listed anxiety, depression, mood lability, insomnia, impaired cognitive functioning, stress and emotional conflicts as among those disturbances that are commonly seen in normal antenatal clinics. Offerman-Zuckerberg (1980) added physical symptoms such as hypertension, excessive nausea, inappropriate weight gain, non-specific pain and cramps in the genital area, fainting, breathing difficulties, digestive upsets and circulation problems, to a similar list.

These psychological and somatic symptoms are remarkably similar to those previously cited as long-term physical and emotional reactions to childhood sexual abuse. Two conclusions can be drawn from this. First, women who have been sexually abused may suffer an increased reaction, thus making their pregnancies a more highly conflicted time. Second, it is conceivable that these symptoms could arouse memories of sexual abuse, thereby increasing the conflicts inherent in pregnancy for a survivor. This may in turn contribute to Courtois' (1991) finding that birth, as a normal developmental event, acts as a trigger to memory retrieval in some survivors.

Experience of Labour and Childhood Sexual Abuse

Leifer (1980), in an intensive descriptive study of nineteen women pregnant for the first time, found that childbirth was overwhelmingly viewed either as a painful ordeal, a 'trial by fire', or as a medical operation. With a dearth of knowledge at the outset, most women in the study invested enormous amounts of energy in learning about birthing, and by the third trimester were well informed, yet still negative or at best ambivalent, about their impending experience.

Most women, therefore, are highly anxious about childbirth (Leifer, 1980). Grossman, et al. (1980) found that doubts about the ability to produce a healthy baby arc notably higher in women with low self-esteem and Young (1984) described some women fearing a loss of identity. Many women feared exposure and giving birth in the presence of strangers (Grossman, et al., 1980; Raphael-Leff, 1980). Increased anxiety and tensions are likely for the sexual abuse survivor.

Fear of loss of control was also reported to be an issue (Grossman, et al., 1980; Kitzinger, 1983; Leifer, 1980; Offerman-Zuckerberg, 1980; Raphael-Leff, 1980). As already described, control is an issue for sexual abuse survivors and it seems likely that this fear would be felt more intensely by them. Similarly, Leifer (1980) and Raphael-Leff (1980) reported a widespread fear of death and loss of consciousness, which is one way of losing control, among pregnant women, in spite of medical advances.

As labour approached, fears around body vulnerability, damage and pain - of being ripped apart or destroyed or of having an episiotomy - were also commonly reported (Grossman, et al., 1980; Leifer, 1980; Offerman-Zuckerberg, 1980). As sexual abuse survivors have previously suffered body traumatization, it is possible that labour may revive old memories and heighten fear and conflicts around this. Their chances of experiencing difficult labour may be increased by fear and tension, and the accompanying physical pain may be overlayed with psychological pain from previous abuse (personal communication, Cheryl Woolley, June 1992).

Leifer (1980) reported that all the women in her study believed that the relationship with their physicians and their trust and confidence in them were crucial. She also reported that women who were not able to maintain control, who screamed or begged for medication, were likely to be disapproved of by staff who preferred labour to follow a predictable routine course. Because the women were vulnerable and dependent, they were more likely to want to please staff, rarely challenging staff and learning quickly which behaviours engendered more positive support.

Medicalization of Labour and its Impact on Survivors of
Childhood Sexual Abuse

The medicalization of childbirth in industrialized societies has been well documented (Kitzinger, 1983; Oakley, 1979). Women have been socialized through most of their lives and during pregnancy to view birth as an illness rather than a natural event (Leifer, 1980). Consequently, the list of medical procedures a woman may have to undergo is long and includes regular antenatal checkups, vaginal examinations throughout pregnancy and labour, ultrasound monitoring, 'prepping' on entry to hospital, the induction of labour through rupture of the membranes or pharmacological preparations, monitoring of uterine contractions and of the foetal heart, insertion of a saline drip, epidural anaesthesia or other pain killing injections, episiotomy and forceps extraction of the baby (Oakley, 1980).

Oakley (1980) wrote that the medical profession, in gearing themselves to lower mortality rates, has failed to take account of in spite of increased attempts in recent years to regard pregnancy as normal. Pregnancy is still widely viewed as a 'condition' with 'symptoms' (Oakley, 1980; Young,˙1984).

Similarly, widespread interventions alienate a woman from her experience in two ways. Firstly, they render her more passive than she need be, and, secondly, her subjective experience is negated or devalued by the use of instruments that objectify her internal experience and move the control over how her birth process is observed from her own self report to the medical staff.

Young (1984) argued that women were further alienated by the hierarchical doctor/patient structure. In addition, most doctors are male and therefore unable to share the 'lived-body experience' - a recognized condition of good medical practice (Pellegrino & Thomsina, 1981, cited in Young, 1984). As well, doctors often need to use distance (Young, 1984) or joking and inflicting discomfort (Oakley, 1979) to desexualize the relationship.

Women, therefore, can be profoundly alienated from their birth experience by their lack of autonomy and control over the process. As a child's experience of sexual abuse can be profoundly alienating, as previously discussed, and as sexual abuse survivors often suffer alienation as a long-term effect, these women may be more susceptible to and affected by any added alienation inherent in their birthing experience.

The Role of Anxiety in Pregnancy and Birthing

Anxiety also plays an important role in pregnancy and childbirth. Anxiety and symptoms of anxiety are well documented as long-term effects of childhood sexual abuse (Browne & Finkelhor, 1986; Mullen, et al., 1988).

Omer and Everly (1988), in a review of studies, concluded that chronic or repetitive (as opposed to acute) stress contribute to pre-term labour. Stress and anxiety have been positively correlated with pre-term and obstetric difficulties in a number of studies (Georgas, et al., 1984; Gorsuch & Key, 1974; Jones, 1978). Similarly, Lederman, et al. (1979) cited a number of studies relating maternal anxiety to dysfunctional and prolonged labour. They explored the relationship between length of labour and the production of enephrine. They measured enephrine levels to gauge the extent of anxiety and suggested that normal physiological mechanisms are impaired through stress-activated emotional/biochemical processes.

Jacobs (1991), in a small retrospective study, examined anxiety and stress during pregnancy and childbirth in sexual abuse survivors. He compared sexual abuse survivors from a treatment programme with a comparison group that did not report childhood sexual abuse. He found that duration of labour in first pregnancy was significantly related to childhood sexual abuse, that sexual abuse survivors perceived themselves as being under greater stress in their first pregnancies, and that higher reported stress in all pregnancies was related to childhood sexual abuse. He commented further on sexual abuse survivors' fears of loss of control as the body took over, and suggested that the physical experience of labour may act as an internal trigger, raising anxiety and therefore interfering with the normal progression of labour.

Jacobs also noted proportionately higher weight gains made by survivors in his study. He suggested that this may reflect increased anxiety, activated by the pregnancy, or the presence of underlying eating disorder issues. An association between eating disorders and childhood sexual abuse has previously been noted.

Although Jacobs' results were preliminary and he acknowledged difficulties in the nature and size of his sample, this study does indicate that childhood sexual abuse may subsequently affect pregnancy and labour. Moreover, the results endorsed other connections noted by Evans, Kotch and Ringwalt (1988, cited in Jacob, 1991) who reported more medical problems during pregnancy and childbirth, and higher rates of premature deliveries in sexual abuse survivors. As their results were part of a larger study focusing on high risk factors for infants, sexual abuse was only one of the possible contributing factors and was not examined more closely.

Boadella (1987) described the physical effect of tension, stress or fear on birthing women. He stated that the sympathetic nervous system becomes dominant in states of stress and tension, causing the 'figure of eight' muscles around the cervix to contract, restricting blood flow and resulting in an increase in pain in nerve endings. This sympathetic action also weakens the contractions of the longitudinal muscles, which nevertheless continue to work as they are primarily governed by hormone release. This means the uterus is trying to perform two mutually antagonistic actions. He likened this to attempting to straighten and bend an arm simultaneously - the muscle goes into spasm and becomes painful.

The presence of anxiety, therefore, increases the risk of difficulties during labour. As previously stated, generalized anxiety is a common long-term effect of childhood sexual abuse and for a number of reasons, including medical procedures and hospital routines, survivors may be more susceptible to heightened anxiety when giving birth. It is therefore likely that sexual abuse survivors have an increased risk of complications during birthing. This may be further complicated if the survivor uses somatization as a coping mechanism.

The Role of Somatization

As previously mentioned, Morrison (1989) reported a strong connection between somatization disorder and childhood sexual abuse. Offerman-Zuckerberg (1980), examining the role psychosomatic symptoms play during pregnancy, wrote that as the uterus - a muscle - reacts like any other set of muscles in the body, it will be affected by states of anger, fear, arousal and sexual excitement. She suggested that somatic symptoms during pregnancy may represent repressed feelings resulting from a lack of emotional expression. Stress is a known influential factor, and it is likely if a woman somatizes prior to pregnancy that she will also somatize when under stress during pregnancy.

Zuckerberg (1972) explored the relationship between the extreme incidence of body symptomatology during pregnancy and unconscious and conscious maternal role conflict and concluded that when there was a discrepancy between conscious and unconscious attitudes, somatic symptoms occurred with the greatest frequency, and excessive worry was high (p.165).

While this study examined only maternal role conflict in relationship to psychosomatic symptoms, it does indicate a possible connection between psychosomatic responses and underlying repressed emotion or conflict.

The role childhood sexual abuse may play in pseudocyesis (i.e. false pregnancy) would seem to support this possibility. Henessey and Polk-Wallace (1990) reported in another small study (n = 5) that all of the cases of pseudocyesis in their clinical practice had a history of childhood sexual abuse. The women presented a clinical picture involving substance abuse, depression, low self-esteem and a diagnosis of borderline personality disorder, a psychiatric diagnosis in which survivors are overly represented. They suggested that the process of reaction formation defended these women against feelings of powerlessness and helplessness, high anxiety, and a sense of being damaged.

Conclusion

The literature specifically linking childhood sexual abuse and later difficulties during pregnancy and birthing is minimal. However, links between childhood sexual abuse and difficulties with sexuality later in life are well documented, as are the characteristics which by their nature sexual experience and the birthing process share. In our culture, for many women, pregnancy and birthing arouse conflicts and feelings that sexual abuse survivors already experience in their everyday lives.

A relationship, therefore, between childhood sexual abuse and later experience of pregnancy and birthing seems likely. The form and extent of this relationship are explored through an exposition of Margaret's life using life history method. The reasons for this choice of method and how it was achieved will be outlined and discussed in the following chapter.

2
Life History Research Process

In general terms, the purpose of this study was to explore one woman's perception of the nature of the relationship between her experience of childhood sexual abuse and sexuality, pregnancy and childbirth. The approach chosen for this exploration was the life history method, as it seemed best suited to the retrospective, exploratory and sensitive nature of the topic.

The Life History Method

Faraday and Plummer (1979, p.785) stated that life history technique is best when used in an exploratory fashion for 'generating concepts, hunches and ideas' because it allows an issue to be viewed from both an individual and a structural level 'within the same field and in relationship to other fields. (p.785) They outlined the advantages of this method, three of which applied particularly to this study.

Life history technique:

(i) grapples with the problem of subjective reality of the individual. It documents the inner experiences of the subject under study, that is, how the person interprets, defines and experiences the world. It lays bare 'the world taken for granted' (p.776) of a person,

(ii) enables a focus on the process of lives and permits ambiguity because it allows for the inconsistency of human experience. It is not concerned with the uniformities and regularities but highlights the 'confusions, ambiguities and contradictions' (p.777) of everyday experience,

(iii) focuses on the totality of experience by locating individuals, firstly, in their overall life experiences and, secondly, within the socio-historic frame work of their time.

In this study then, the experience of one person, Margaret, is explored from a number of perspectives, including intrapsychic, interpersonal and socio-historic.

A unique feature of life history method is that it acknowledges the influence of the researcher's subjectivity; that this can be a positive influence and can add to the force of the research (McRobbie, 1982). The method is composed of the subject's story and the researcher's analysis of that story. Because the researcher's analysis is openly acknowledged as an interpretive act, its existence highlights the possibility of different interpretations and, therefore, suggests that there is no one 'right' or 'real' account. There are also, in any life history narrative, a number of other stories and levels of stories - some told, some untold. There are, for example, the subject's story as told, those parts of the story the subject requests not be told, and the stories of others whose lives intersect with the subject's life (Armstrong, 1991; Faraday & Plummer, 1979).

The crucial problem then, is that of interpretation, the extent to which the researcher imposes his or her constructs upon the understandings of the subject, or the extent to which the subject's own rational construction of the world is apprehended in its purest form (Faraday & Plummer, 1979, p.786).

Faraday and Plummer postulated a 'continuum of contamination' with the subject's pure account, such as diaries and letters at one end and the researcher's 'pure account', written from a theoretical base, at the other. Less extreme positions, such as an edited personal document or systematic thematic analysis, exists in between. Movement through any stage of this continuum is legitimate, as long as the position taken is publicly acknowledged.

The results of this research have been recorded as a biography of Margaret's life. As this is Margaret's story, told mainly in her own words and presented generally in the form that it was shared, it lies somewhere between an edited personal document, with minimum intervention from the researcher, and a thematic analysis, where data would have been considerably sorted and reorganized by the researcher.

Life history method lays no claim to representativeness (Faraday & Plummer, 1979; Shostak, 1989). It is not primarily concerned with 'objectivity'. All life history narratives involve 'selective recall' (Geiger, 1986, p.347) and are concerned with trying to grasp 'personal' truth rather than 'universal' truth. This does not mean, however, that there may not be elements of things universal within them. Because of the in-depth nature of the current exploration and the lack of research in this area, it was decided in this study that only one subject would be interviewed. There was, therefore, no broad base with which to compare personal bias and distance from statistical norms.

Because the area under study was so sensitive, it was particularly important to use methodology that was collaborative and if possible empowering (Lather, 1991). Life history, as a participatory process (Geiger, 1986), can achieve this. Margaret agreed to read and comment on the results and the final contents of the biography required her approval. This enabled her to maintain some control and power over this personally revealing document.

There were also a number of times when, as she remembered experiences, Margaret herself made connections previously unconsidered. This happened most noticeably after she recalled the experience of her first birth and the important part breathing played in that. At this point she became excited even astounded by the connections she had made and said:

'That feels like a little bit of my jigsaw has fitted into place.'

Life histories then reveal the link between experience and consciousness and help us see that consciousness is not simply the act of interpreting our world, but also of constructing it (Stanley & Wise, in Geiger, 1986). Shostak (1989) wrote:

'No more elegant tool exists to describe the human condition than the personal narrative. Ordinary people living ordinary and not so ordinary lives weave from their memories and experiences the meaning life has for them.' (p.239)

When producing a personal narrative using life history methodology it is important, therefore, to consider the conditions in which it is created, the forms that guide it and the relationship that produces it.

The Research Relationship and the Role of the Researcher

Personal narratives do not exist independently of the collaborative process involved in their collection (Shostak, 1989). Faraday and Plummer (1979) have discussed the difficulties that can arise from this. They wrote that the research basis of the relationship can at times become ambiguous, given the personal nature of the material and the possibility that this is its first disclosure. Also, due to the unstructured nature of the interviews, an explicit contract regarding how often to meet or the extent of involvement is difficult to define from the beginning. The positive aspects of the relationship are the possibilities for providing emotional support, hospitality and the reassurance to subjects 'that they are not alone'. (p.790) The biggest advantage Faraday and Plummer described, however, was the possibility that the autobiography presented at the completion of the project be 'essentially a memoir through which they [the subjects] will have the power publicly to present their own definitions' (p.790) of their experience.

Life history method, therefore, involves the researcher and the subject in an intense and intimate relationship (Faraday & Plummer, 1979). I had known Margaret prior to beginning this research. The advantage of this was that rapport was already created and trust established, which enabled Margaret to share personal aspects of her life fully. However, this also meant that potential for the research basis of the relationship becoming unclear was increased. Margaret and I had no social contact over this time, to help keep the research relationship as 'clear' as possible. Clarity was assisted by the process used to set up the research, outlined in the following section, and by Margaret having talked and written about much of the material before as part of her recovery process.

Our interviews, however, were relaxed and informal. Because life history methodology is a participatory process, it addresses the hierarchical relationship that can exist between the researcher and the researched (Geiger, 1986). Oakley (1981) described an interview as an interaction between two people each with unique personality traits and interests at a particular time in life and that this needs to be acknowledged and reflected in any presentation. The interviews with Margaret were based on our relationship and our shared common experience. Throughout the interviews, when Margaret described the impact of sexual abuse on her life there were times when I had experienced a similar response or event and I briefly shared this with her.

The advantage of this was that the level of rapport established enabled personal issues to be addressed at a deep level without this experience becoming abusive of Margaret. The difficulty for me as the researcher involved separating out my own experience and responses. It was important to maintain a boundary around these that was neither too rigid and inflexible, which might damage the in-depth nature of the communication, nor too permeable resulting in undue influence over the nature of the data collected and the direction in which it developed.

This appropriate boundary was accomplished in part by the unstructured nature of the interviews which, as Brannen (1988) suggested, allows the subject more control. Margaret led the process, beginning her story where she chose, allowing it to unfold naturally with minimal intervention. Sometimes I asked questions. This was generally in order to clarify some point or to go more deeply into a particular subject. For example, the fourth interview began with the clarification of a point from the previous interview. This lead to Margaret talking of the pain she used to experience after intercourse. I queried then whether she suffered from any recurring infections such as thrush. Margaret initially indicated not but as she spoke of the discomfort considered that it might have been thrush and said *'knowing me I wouldn't have gone [to the doctor] anyway for that area'*. Queries about other gynaecological problems were made, to which Margaret answered *'Oh no ... well... come to think of it...'* and went on to describe the considerable difficulties she had experienced for years around menstruation.

The Subject

The research required the subject be a childhood sexual abuse survivor who had subsequently given birth to at least one child. The birth needed to have occurred prior to any sexual abuse recovery work undertaken by the subject so that the relationship between the abuse issues and the birth experiences remained uncontaminated. For ethical reasons it was important the subject planned to have no more children and had worked through major issues in relation to the sexual abuse she experienced, so that the risk of the research process activating unresolved issues was minimized.

I had made Margaret's acquaintance six years before and had had intermittent contact with her subsequently. Knowing something of her circumstances, I approached her as a possible subject in April 1992.

Initial Proposal and Setting Up the Project

At the first meeting the nature of the research was outlined, including the requirements of a subject, my own stance regarding subjectivity and objectivity and the construction of knowledge, the nature of life history as a method and the intention that the research be collaborative and involve both mutuality and reciprocity.

Difficulties that could be foreseen were discussed. The issue of anonymity, the likely time commitment given the nature of the research and the possibility that retelling her story might revive old feelings and conflicts, were covered. Safeguards within the research, addressed in the following section on ethical concerns, were outlined, including her right to exit at any time, the opportunity for further counselling from another individual should it be required, and the contents of the biography material and the availability of the research being decided in consultation with her.

Margaret then took time to think about the implications of her participation for herself and her family, and to discuss it with them. She was contacted again one week later and some of the information was repeated. At this time Margaret was feeling positive about the possibility of participating. She spoke of her hope that she might contribute something and receive something herself from the process, as it might fit together some of her memories. She queried whether her previous memory loss about much of her childhood would present a problem. As all memory recall is selective, it was decided that it would not.

On the 29th of April Margaret received a copy of the research proposal for her to consider further her involvement. Finally, on May 26th, I met with Margaret at her work . She had agreed to participate and we discussed how we would organize the process. By this time Margaret's partner David had left to work overseas for a number of months and Margaret expressed anxiety about the time frame of the research. She hoped to join him later in the year and had examinations to sit herself in October. She also expressed anxiety about the whole process saying, *'When I read it [the proposal] I felt scared and put it under my pillow'*. More than once she said thoughtfully that a connection between sexual abuse and birthing had never occurred to her but that she had had a very long labour with her first born. She was very clear, however, about wanting to participate.

Ethical Issues

A number of ethical issues arose due to both the sensitive nature of the issues being addressed and the use of life history methodology.

Brannen (1988) discussed the issues raised by studies of sensitive topics and the disclosure of personal and confidential information. Firstly, subjects can often easily be identified due to the unique and personal nature of the information given. This is particularly the case with life history technique (Shostak, 1989) where only a degree of anonymity can ever be accomplished. This was particularly problematic for Margaret as her being a twin made her more easily identifiable. She had also previously participated in a radio programme on sexual abuse. Informed consent was therefore crucial and these limitations were fully discussed with Margaret prior to her initial agreement to participate. Her agreement was sought again at the end of the research.

Subjects in studies on sensitive topics also often find confronting and telling their stories a stressful experience (Brannen, 1988). Because Margaret had worked extensively on these issues previously, this likelihood was lessened. However, the option of further counselling from another person being available was discussed and provided for, and Margaret's right to exit from the research at any time without prejudice remained an option throughout.

Another ethical issue Brannen (1988) highlighted, is that subjects who disclose personal, sensitive material are vulnerable to the way in which data is interpreted. However, by using a participatory process, which life history provides (Geiger, 1986), the subject and the researcher are able to collaborate and Margaret, therefore, had control over the content and form of the presentation of the data. As previously discussed, unstructured interviews also allow subjects some control (Brannen, 1988). Similarly, the researcher's discussion of the life history needs

'to be in terms of the analytic and epistemological implications of the life, not the intricacies of bizarre, individual behaviour.'
(Armstrong, 1991)

Timing and Setting of Interviews

The method involved in-depth, unstructured interviews with one subject about her life experience. Likely themes were picked up and focused on and included:

(i) the family context,
(ii) the experience of the sexual abuse and the recovery process,
(iii) sexuality,
(iv) experiences of giving birth.

Margaret was interviewed seven times in total. The initial five interviews took place between the fourth and the twenty fifth of June 1992 and over this time Margaret told her story as she recalled it. Each interview was taped and took place either in Margaret's or the researcher's home.

The interviews were between one hour and one-and-a-quarter hours long, except for the fifth interview which was about one-and-three-quarter hours in length. The interviews were informal, often shared over a cup of tea, and unstructured. At times I asked for clarification or for more information. In the main, Margaret spoke of her life as she remembered it. At times she laughed, at other times she spoke quietly with a distant look, and sometimes she was sad and seemed wistful.

Margaret was working during June when most of the interviews took place. Her husband, David, was overseas and she was living alone. She arrived for the first interview having just *'put herself together,'* as she described it, having recently heard that a close friend had cancer.

Margaret admitted at the beginning of the third interview that she was not sleeping well but she was not sure if this was connected to the research or not. She talked of being so busy that she 'mainly shoved it down out of the way'. Margaret was very tired throughout this interview which dealt mainly with her sexuality and sexual relationship with David. She spoke sadly at the end of two friends who were both dying of cancer and of her fears of David dying. She appeared to have a heightened sense of David's mortality and was missing him very much. It was evident there was an enormous sense of loss and grief, both present and past, about the things she and David had lost or not been able to share until recently in their relationship.

The Research Process

After each interview the tapes were partially transcribed. Careful and repeated listening between interviews provided points for clarification and development at the start of the next interview, in order to allow ongoing comment on accuracy. However, this tended to distract from the natural flow and it proved better for Margaret to begin by picking up from where she was, leaving clarification for later.

From the end of June until October 12th, when the sixth interview took place, Margaret and I had no contact. Over this time, literature on birthing and pregnancy in particular was explored. Margaret sat her examinations, David returned and they celebrated their twenty fifth wedding anniversary and organized their daughter's twenty first birthday.

The sixth interview was more structured, in that Margaret was asked questions relating to her pregnancy and her relationships in particular. She then moved into talking of her experience carrying out cervical smears and her reactions to this. Margaret seemed more aware and self observant of her physical and emotional responses around these subjects at this time and it seemed possible that this resulted from her participation in the research.

While this stance was particularly evident in this interview, further listening and analysis of the previously taped interviews highlighted Margaret's increasing awareness of the extent to which the trauma of her childhood and her responses to it had and were still affecting her later experiences. This awareness was evident on numerous occasions and on a variety of topics. For example, as Margaret recalled her growing relationship with David, she began to comment on and was surprised by the extent of their lack of physical closeness. Again, she initially said she had had no gynaecological problems but then revised this saying, *'Come to think of it...'* and spoke of the pain she experienced as a girl at menstruation and later linked that pain with pain she experienced after sexual intercourse.

The seventh and final interview took place on 29th of November. The aim was for Margaret to read her story, to make any connections or note anything important that might have been omitted and for her to give feedback on the life history. Margaret asked me to read the biography to her as she felt she would be unable to concentrate if she read it herself. She would *'switch out'*. Some minor changes, for example how Margaret felt as a child in church, were made in order to depict more accurately Margaret's experience. One point Margaret felt strongly about was the description of PKF (the abuser). For her, it was very important to include the froth at the corner of PKF's mouth:

'This was almost the worst bit... it was one of the things I hated most.'

Interestingly, Margaret had never mentioned this before but it was clearly very important for her and needed to be included. It emphasized the importance and value of taking time to go over the narrative together.

Conclusion

This Chapter has discussed life history method as a research process and the role of the researcher and the research relationship in this method. The participatory nature of this method has been described, including the importance of the initial proposal, the setting up of the project and how, when and where the data was collected. Ethical concerns have also been addressed.

3
Margaret's Story

This chapter presents Margaret's story, wherever possible using her own words. The story follows her life generally in chronological order, with particular focus on her experience of sexual abuse, sexuality, pregnancy and birthing.

At the time of the interviews Margaret was forty six years old. She was working full-time as a General Practice Nurse and her two children, Jane and Ruth, were twenty three and twenty one respectively. Jane was newly married. Margaret's husband, David, was overseas on business and Margaret told proudly of their plans to celebrate twenty five years of marriage on his return.

Early History

Margaret's mother, the eldest in her family, was responsible for her much younger sister and two brothers. They grew up in small town New Zealand during the Depression. She left school early to work as a domestic and often went into homes when the mother of the family was away having a baby. Margaret's mother told her later of the difficulties she encountered with some of the husbands, *'sometimes respectable people who were friends of my parents'*, who would try to take advantage of her as she looked after their young children. *'It was a secret all those years'*. She had told no one because she needed the work. Margaret's mother was 10 years younger than her husband. *'She was a good home mum'*, following her husband *'dutifully and willingly'* when he moved the family for his work. Margaret *'had a good relationship [with her mother] and could talk about most things with her'*.

Margaret's father had a brief childless marriage before marrying Margaret's mother and paid maintenance to his first wife for twenty years. He felt some shame around this and had never wanted his children to know; they were told just a few days before he died. As a child Margaret never understood why they had so little money. Her memories of her father were of him *'working very, very hard down at his office or behind his desk in the lounge, shut away behind the door'*. Her father, while working in a dairy factory, completed his accountancy exams. His first job as an accountant took the family to Christchurch, when Margaret was four years old.

Margaret's brother, John, was born two years after her parents' marriage when her mother was twenty six. Twenty two months later her mother gave birth to twin girls. The birth was difficult, both were breach, and Margaret, the smaller, was born second.

Early Childhood

Margaret had a few memories of her early life. She had leg splints and was hot in bed at night. Margaret wanted her Mum to cut her hair, but her father would not allow it. Margaret remembered a train ride from Lyttelton to Christchurch, *'It was a big, big frost. It was so heavy a frost it was like snow. It was magic!'*

Margaret did not remember much of her childhood from this point on. She had *'been told bits of it'*, and as she remembered some aspects has had these verified by her sister Mary and by her mother. Mary remembered their childhood well, *'She has been my memory in many ways.'* Margaret recalled her frustration at not remembering and worrying why she did not. During conversations when her mother and sister reminisced, Margaret, not wanting to feel excluded, would pretend that she did remember.

Margaret and Mary, although not identical, had always been very close. Margaret spoke of them often having feelings when each of them knew what was happening for the other. This felt *'neat'* for Margaret, *'really special'*.

The sexual abuse started in these early years in Christchurch. *'I figure it started when I was about six and went on till I was about fourteen'*. Margaret was abused by a close friend of her father - PKF she called him. At this time Margaret's father was the *'top dog in the Masons, Grand Worshipful Master, or some such thing,'* and had to go away frequently. Her father's friend, also a Mason and an older man, took the twins on picnics, partly as company for his granddaughter and partly as a break for Margaret's mother. He never took Margaret's brother.

The abuse began with what Margaret called, *'unpleasant but not invasive stuff'*, inappropriate touching of her breasts and more often her genital area and tongue kissing. This was the extent of the abuse when the three children were present. Mary remembered being touched as they drove in the car and the tongue kisses when they had to kiss him 'thank you'.

Mary then developed asthma, began to be sick frequently with pneumonia and, therefore, was no longer able to go on the outings. *'She used to cry and say, "Don't let Margaret go"'*. Margaret's mother, thinking Mary was disappointed, would point out the unfairness of making Margaret miss out because Mary was sick. If Margaret protested, her mother would think she was *'sticking up for Mary ... So off I would go'*. But when there was only Margaret and no Mary, PKF no longer picked up his grand-daughter;

> *'He only took me... The abuse then became more intense, violent and sadistic. When I was on my own he would want me to touch him and I didn't want to do it. I had this inborn belief that it was wrong, so I resisted. He used to change... It was as if he became a different person. He'd get angry...When he got really angry he got really violent. I didn't have any option. I was really frightened... He would tie me up. He used to take me to forests out of Christchurch and he would tie me up to a tree. It seemed to tickle his fancy to do it in different ways. It was quite bizarre sometimes tied with my hands behind the tree and my feet together... so just standing upright... sometimes kneeling down and then a noose thing strung up over the tree and round my neck, so that I had to kneel up tall. If I sagged down, which of course you do when you get tired, it pulled on the thing round my neck until I'd agree to do what he wanted... He'd tie me up to get me to agree... He made me do a handstand up against the tree and then he'd tie one leg up - just one so the other one got pretty tired... Half the time he'd just stand and stare.*
>
> *He had this fruit knife in the car... it had a sheath...a long thin fruit knife ... and sometimes he'd just stand and look at that and turn it over in his hand. I don't think he ever cut me with it, but just him doing that while he looked at me was awful. He'd tell me to undress, and eventually I had to and sometimes he'd just stand and look at me. Sometimes he'd tie me [on the ground] between the trees - stretched out sort of - starfish, you know - he really was quite bizarre. Usually [I was tied] until I'd agree to do whatever he wanted. And sometimes he actually forced himself on me then, while I was tied up in that way on the ground. After he'd raped me he told me to go and wash myself in the river. It was by a river. And then he wouldn't let me get dressed until he told me I could.'*

Margaret did not remember all that happened to her, but from the recovery process work she did she knew she was raped rectally, vaginally and orally.

Sometimes the same sorts of things happened in his home. He would take all three girls to his home and make popcorn and toffee apples and *'it was quite fun'*. Often, after those outings, Margaret would be treated to a big bag of acid drops and raspberry drops. Later, as the abuse intensified, threats of what he would do to her twin were enough to keep Margaret quiet:

> *'The sorts of things he was doing to me, he said he would do to Mary, and I knew she wouldn't survive what he was doing to me. In*

my childlike way, because she was so sick now, having trouble breathing, she wouldn't have been able to breathe doing what he was doing.'

Coping Strategies

Margaret's mother remembered her suddenly becoming very private, and on her return home from these outings Margaret would go down to a hut behind the shed in her backyard. There she had:

'a little toy dog made of sheepskin and I used to just [curl up and] cuddle that.... I would put myself back together. Or I would go into the bathroom and I was in there a long time.... I'd lock the door. I used to have a really good wash - take all my clothes off and wash. Mum recalls me being in there for long spells at a time.'

Margaret used to hide any signs of the abuse, *'I used to wear skivvies that covered my neck and my wrists and long trousers that covered my ankles.'*

Margaret's mother also remembered coming into Margaret's bedroom and finding her head first under the bedclothes at the bottom of her bed. She thought Margaret was having a bad dream, but Margaret was actually practising breathing. PKF used to put things over her face when he raped her, and when he orally raped her that for her was more frightening because she couldn't breathe. About that time, in the newspapers, there was a little Australian boy, David Thorpe, who had been sexually abused and left in the boot of a car. He had been suffocated and Margaret was determined that that would not happen to her:

'There were the times when he used to suffocate me when I didn't have control over it. But, basically, I had this belief as a child that if I practised hard enough, he couldn't do that anymore. And so breathing became almost my key to survival. If I practised hard enough, then, even if he did have something over my face, he wouldn't smother me... that is when I used to practise down in bed with the pillows and everything piled on top of me and practise breathing when I had a heavy weight all over my face. Everything was down under the bed clothes... I'd lie down on the bed and I'd have my pillows on me and then the blankets and that, just all tucked tightly pressing down... trying to redo the sorts of things he'd done but proving to myself that I could still breathe... I think I did it in all sorts of ways.'

Margaret also learned to protect herself by dissociating from her body:

'About the time of the actual abuse, I actually learned to hold my breathe till I passed out... I used to hold my breathe till everything just... I realize now I passed out... There were times when I hadn't any control so I decided I'd learn how to still be able to breathe and then breathing became important. Yeah, and then I

learned this way of actually dissociating - stop breathing till I passed out... I remember when I did come back, he'd just be standing there, not actually touching me. He'd just stand there and stare - look. I think I got to the stage that's how I always dealt with it. I just passed out... disconnected myself in some way through my breathing.'

Margaret remembered aspects of her school days. She was a very busy girl, loved lunch time and played sport frequently. In Standard Two she was called 'wettie pants' - she hated to be the focus of attention and if brought to the front of the class or asked to read aloud, would wet her pants. Mary was her best friend and the friends she brought home were *'the outcasts and the poor ones.'* Margaret always wanted to be a nurse:

'Being able to help people made me feel better...made me feel good... my whole life just about was involved with helping people feel better - all the waifs and the strays and the little hedgehogs and anything else I picked up and tried to fix.'

She was apparently a *'regular chatterbox,'* and recalled her father irritatedly saying *'"Yap! yap! yap! yap! yap!" So I must have gone on a bit'*. However, while Margaret would chat about anything else, she did not disclose her secret. As she was being abused she was told she wasn't allowed to make any noise.

'I was told I wasn't allowed to... I was actually told not to make any noise - I had to be quiet or else - and I presumed the 'or else' meant it would be worse. I wasn't allowed to be sick if I was heaving or after he'd come in my mouth. I couldn't be sick, I wanted to vomit, I had to swallow. There was no way I could make a noise or be sick or anything. It just wasn't allowed. I guess I didn't dare... If I did anything wrong, he would get so angry and then it would be worse. If he was angry, he was far more violent and sadistic than if he wasn't, so it was better not to rock the boat. When he was angry his eyes would pop out, the veins on his neck would stand up... he used to get this froth on the corner of his mouth... and his face would go purple - revolting, and I was just frightened stiff... I just couldn't tell anybody. 'Cos if I did, Mary would get it and it would be worse. So that part of me had to be silent.'

So Margaret remained quiet:

'Partly not to anger him further, either way so as not to hurt more, either me or my sister.'

Margaret also began bedwetting, sleepwalking and had terrible nightmares. She had a recurring nightmare of a person, like a joker from a pack of cards, with a triangular face and a wide open mouth, sitting cross-legged in the right hand corner of her room. He would be laughing and laughing. On waking, she could not breathe nor move and she would try and call out to her mother, but no sound would come out. Then everything would go black and she would pass out, before resuming breathing and waking properly. She could not call out, even to Mary in the bed next to her. She could not make a sound.

Margaret learned in time, however, to have her own dream which she could *'switch into'* at will. In her dream, she would fly around the world and rescue people from floods and other disasters. She towed these people behind her with a piece of rope. This became a serial dream which she could continue at will, picking up from where she had left it:

> *'It was very powerful in a nice sort of way and I guess it was one way I could go to bed.'*

Margaret used to delay going to bed. She remembers pretending to her parents that she was going, but instead she stayed up. Sometimes, in the fourth and fifth form, she worked on homework until the early hours of the morning.

As she grew older, sport became her means of escape from PKF. By the time she went to high school, she played cricket all day on Saturdays. In Winter, she played hockey for a club and for school and indoor basketball for the school and at representative level. She played as many as five games a day including practices, and was no longer available for picnics.

Both twins needed to repeat School Certificate. In the third and fourth forms Margaret struggled at school and she was bottom of her class. Although she spent much of her time at her desk working, she managed to learn little. She *'came right'* in her repeated fifth form year. She *'flew through the second time'* and attributed this partly to the abuse having stopped. Later, in her nursing training, she was top of her year group.

From the time the abuse stopped, Margaret suppressed all memories of it. She has become aware that there were a number of ways she did this. She would:

> *'...go flat stick all day, and then I'd drop off to sleep very quickly... I still do it a bit... I'll stop going flat stick and I'm out like a light pretty quickly. I don't have that twilight dreaming, thinking time... It's been bad enough that I've been sitting playing the piano or the organ and I'll actually drop off to sleep and I've fallen off the stool...'*

Margaret had never been able to relax in the bath, as she would go to sleep immediately only to wake up with cold water lapping around her face. When she was nursing, she would fill the bath to the top and pull the plug when she got in. She still sometimes wakes up cold in an empty bath, *'Relaxing wasn't a word I knew... I would just go, go, go - asleep.'*

Margaret had always found it difficult to read as she would fall asleep after reading just a few lines. Studying was, therefore, difficult. She managed to study as a nurse by working with a friend. Each took turns to read and then taught the other.

Sexuality

Margaret denied herself any knowledge or awareness of her sexuality as she moved into adolescence. When her mother tried to talk to her about menstruation and 'things', Margaret was not interested. In fact she would not listen. Her mother has told her since that she *'just about tore her hair out'* as Margaret developed physically yet asked nothing about her maturation or sexuality and showed no interest in talking about it. Although Mary asked her mother questions, Margaret had none. Margaret's mother, in answering Mary's curiosity, actually asked Mary to repeat the same questions when Margaret was there to hear them. She left pamphlets about for Margaret but Margaret resolutely

'didn't want to know. I just didn't want to know anything about anything sexual at all...even very recently... I'd been nursing, I couldn't tell you what a homosexual was or a lesbian was, I mean anything sexual I just shut right out of my mind... I was completely illiterate about some of that stuff as far as what I should have known... I just didn't take it in.'

A number of times in her nursing career, when she was confronted with male sexuality, Margaret panicked. She recalled nursing paraplegics in the Spinal Unit where she had to put in place an appliance to catch the urine. She remembered one man unexpectedly having an erection. Totally shocked and frightened, Margaret simply left the Ward. She could not remember ever doing this particular job again and believed she probably avoided it. Another time she nursed an old man who would slide down onto the floor and would need to be picked up. He would grab at the nurses' breasts as they helped him. Margaret hated it, *'It was just awful.'* She left him until last always and finally refused to assist him. She angrily gave him a pillow and blanket and told him he could stay there until someone else moved him.

Her worst experience, however, occurred years later in Masterton. She was working night shifts in the Coronary Care Unit of the hospital. There were usually only two or three patients and only one intensive care patient at a time. Therefore, the nurses worked alone. One night she was nursing a heart attack patient who had uneven heart rhythms and needed frequent intravenous injections to stay alive. One time, as Margaret gave him the injection, he grabbed her, pulled her onto the bed and began ripping at her uniform. Shocked, Margaret managed eventually to struggle free and rang for help. No one came. She was terrified. Soon after, he went again into the uneven rhythm and needed another injection. Margaret seriously considered leaving him as she was so scared to go near him. Eventually she managed to administer the drug by crawling under the bed and giving it to him from there. She told no one about this incident.

Within a few days she began to have bizarre symptoms. Her vision and speech were affected. She lost control of her bladder, was very tired and weak and had difficulty walking. Margaret told a friend she believed she had a brain tumour. The friend then went to Margaret's doctor who saw Margaret and referred her to a neurologist. The diagnosis was disseminated sclerosis (now commonly called multiple sclerosis). Margaret became depressed and was placed on anti-depressants, refusing to believe she had disseminated sclerosis. She needed home help, but managed to work a little.

When the family moved from Masterton, about fifteen to eighteen months later, Margaret's symptoms immediately began to improve and the disseminated sclerosis was thought to be in remission. Margaret had no recurrence of these symptoms until she was in counselling and began remembering her childhood. The same symptoms, in a milder form, recurred during sessions and went away spontaneously, usually after a few hours. It was only then she connected their onset with her nursing experience.

As an adolescent, Margaret also denied and repressed any sexual feelings. She had few encounters with boyfriends, and those she did have continued only if she perceived them more as friendships than as likely sexual relationships.

Margaret's earliest involvement with a boy was when she was twelve or thirteen. She met him at a family camp. She remembered feeling comfortable holding hands with him. She thought of this more as a friendship. Then, when they were about fifteen, Margaret and Mary went out as a foursome with two boys. They went to dances, biking to and from these together. This relationship also was *'more of a friendship - free from any pressures.'*

However, a friend of her brother called Alan, who was often in their home, fell in love with her. He would ask her out and wrote her very romantic letters. He was older than Margaret - a third year university student. Margaret could not handle the relationship. Unable to tell him assertively how she felt, she resorted to being 'nasty' and contrary, avoiding him and making excuses when he asked her out. Although she recognized him as trustworthy, she felt scared of being alone with him, *'my whole being reacted against him.'* It was a miserable time for her. Unable to explain her fear, she blamed herself and felt terribly guilty. *'He finally got the message,'* not long before his final exams and was so unhappy that he *'failed all his third year papers.'*

Margaret had met David by this time. They were in the same study group at a national Christian Camp held annually at Christmas. *'It was very gentle and not in any way sexual.'* Then, one Easter when Margaret was sixteen or seventeen and at the time that Alan was pursuing her, Margaret met David again at another youth camp. David was obviously interested in Margaret and she *'thought he was a nice guy.'* He had no expectation of holding her hand or kissing her goodnight.

> *'I felt fine with him but I just saw it as a friendship. Most of the time we were in opposite islands. It was a relationship that grew through letter writing and there wasn't much physical closeness at all.'*

Margaret completed the sixth form and on leaving school took a number of temporary jobs until she was eighteen and old enough to start nursing. She went to the North Island briefly and stayed with her grandparents in Palmerston North. Every weekend David drove over to see her, and once she went back to Wanganui and spent the weekend with his family. Margaret *'didn't mind going home in the car with him.'* She had no memory of any sexual aspect to their relationship at this time. She was *'still only just thinking of him as a friend.'* Margaret remembered feeling comfortable and safe in David's company and not feeling threatened. She did not remember any sexual contact with him and thought it most likely they had none.

Following another Easter camp, David left for mission work in Vanuatu and Margaret started nursing. Margaret remembered feeling sad and thought at this time she began to think of him as her boyfriend. Certainly other people did, as she and David were the subject of mild teasing by their friends.

Margaret remembered it was from Vanuatu that David began starting his letters *'"My Dear Margaret,"'* and putting kisses on them, *'and that was actually O.K.! [laughs] I suppose it was still safe. It was on paper.'* Margaret and David wrote to one another most days - ongoing twenty to thirty page letters. They did *'a lot of talking'* in these letters and *'got to know each other very well.'*

Margaret's nursing holidays coincided with David completing his mission work. While David had been lent a book on romance and marriage by friends at the mission, Margaret was still oblivious to this possibility and *'nothing about that was said in the letters.'* The Church paid for David to visit Australia and speak about his work before he returned home. It also arranged for Margaret to join him there and for them to holiday together, staying with church people. It was a special time, *'all very clean and above board.'* David proposed to Margaret there and Margaret who, *'honestly wasn't thinking any sexual thoughts at all'*, accepted.

Married Life

As she prepared for her wedding, Margaret remained oblivious to the sexual aspects of marriage:

> *'In those days it was traditional for brides to have a white*

nightie. I bought pink and only because I needed one! I don't think I had any actual romantic build up. By then I think we probably held hands and had the odd kiss, but I didn't think of what it might lead to. .. that sort of thing... it didn't enter my mind.'

It apparently did enter Margaret's mother's mind; she suggested Margaret see a gynaecologist for a check-up before the wedding. Margaret did not remember much about it, but thought it was probably because she had never asked anything and her mother wanted to be sure everything was normal and Margaret was as informed as possible. The gynaecologist tried to examine Margaret internally but was unable to do so. He gave Margaret a plastic dilator, *'so presumably I was a bit tense.'* Margaret never used it.

On the first night of her honeymoon, in a motel in Christchurch, Margaret fainted:

> *'I don't remember the getting ready to go to bed or anything...*
> *do remember my heart absolutely racing... and I can remember what*
> *seemed to me like incredible pain and then passing out.'*

They tried again the next night, but it was no better and Margaret thought they probably gave up then.

She remembered that when they tried to have sex, possibly a month or two later, she woke on her feet from a nightmare, shouting that the house was on fire, *'So it must have been stirring me up a bit.'* Margaret spoke of never wanting to have sex:

> *'I was never keen... I must have been like a lump of lead. I certainly*
> *dreaded it and I would never do anything to entice him. Sometimes*
> *it was months between... which is pretty sad when I think about it.*
> *For years I hated it. I'd go to bed as late as I could.'*

Margaret suffered from dyspareunia. Intercourse always hurt, although the nurse in her knew to use a lubricant:

> *'It was always painful and yet it needn't have been... must have just*
> *been tension with me, I think. Even after Jane was born... it shouldn't*
> *have been painful then ... I should have been stretched.'*

Margaret could only manage to have sex in two positions. Both lacked intimacy, and as Margaret described them she sadly said, *'You couldn't get much further away.'* Either she lay on her stomach hugging a pillow facing away and slightly curled up, or they lay almost on their backs *'like a pair of scissors'* with their heads as far apart as possible, only their legs entwined. Margaret could never bear to have David's body on hers, *'It felt too much like a suffocating pressure.'* Margaret found kissing on the lips provoked feelings of suffocation. Oral sex had never been possible. She used a form of dissociation to enable her to manage any sexual contact:

> *'I think probably right from the start I used to just space out - not*
> *be present... We'd be in the middle of it and I'd start talking about*

*something absolutely unrelated like what the kids had said. I think
I just lay there... I never did any giving, that's for sure... as far as the
sexual side went, I never gave a thing I realize now.'*

She also had no form of arousal:

*'The way I coped best was as quick as possible. In and out and then
out to the bathroom... I always got straight up and had a wash like
mad. None of this nice romantic lying and sleeping business... I'd
take my time doing that and he'd be asleep by the time I came back.'*

Although David was the most patient of partners, Margaret thought
he found this particularly hard. Margaret, however, told no one of the
difficulties she had with sex. She remembered speaking with Mary about
the dyspareunia after Mary, who also suffered from it, raised the topic.

Margaret's vaginal area would hurt and feel raw after intercourse.
She also had a *'real dragging ache for several days'* in her lower abdomen
that was *'really uncomfortable.'* This happened until after counselling just
a few years ago. Margaret found it hard to understand this and thought it
was due to her tension:

*'Certainly it was a physical feeling of pain and discomfort... in a
sense it is not terribly logical to have the discomfort I had after such
a short...[laugh]. I guess I didn't know it wasn't normal for other
people to feel like that too...[laugh].'*

Margaret did not remember having any vaginal infections. Thrush, for
example, can cause a raw burning sensation following intercourse:

*'I would be uncomfortable, and whether that was a thrush infection
and I didn't do anything about it... I'm not aware of having to go
and have treatments for things, but then, knowing me, I wouldn't
have gone anyway for that area.'*

Prior to her sexual abuse counselling, when she *'became as regular as
clockwork'*, Margaret had always had very irregular periods - anything from
twenty to fifty days apart. Margaret used to have severe pain the first day of
menstruation. The pain was in her lower abdomen and cramping inside her
vagina with backache. It was so severe she would vomit with the pain, and
when she was nursing she recalled fainting - not from the loss of blood, as she
lost little on her first day, but from the pain. Other staff, thinking she had
appendicitis would want to get the doctor and have her admitted:

*'I knew it wasn't that... it used to be so embarrassing that everybody
was trying to do all these heroics, and I just wanted to go away and
curl up with a hot water bottle... be left alone. So I remember that
very clearly, because I used to have such a battle with them not to
get the doctor.'*

Margaret had had this same pain since her high school days. When she was
younger, a doctor she was taken to see had patted her hand and said that when

she grew up and had a baby, it would come right. It did not improve. Although Mary did not suffer from period pain to this extent, Margaret never thought to question her own experience:

> *'It was normal for me...I don't ever remember thinking, "Why me?" about anything. I don't think it's a question I would ever ask.'*

Pregnancy

When Margaret and David had been married about two and a half years, they decided to have a baby. They *'didn't have to try hard'* and they made love seldom enough for Margaret to know when she conceived:

> *'It was funny. Both times conceived as planned. It was first pop both times... each time we decided we will and we did.'*

Margaret was about twenty four and a nursing tutor when she became pregnant with Jane. She had severe morning sickness for a number of months - feeling sick all day and into the evening. She vomited a lot and her *'tummy popped out'* very quickly as she carried extra fluid around the baby. There was some concern that Margaret might have been developing diabetes as she had a very high reading (two percent) of sugar in her urine: *'I wasn't. I was eating a lot of sugar... too much for my kidneys to cope and it spilled over into my urine.'* She also had severe pain in her genital area:

> *'I just thought it was because I was expanding... it felt like I was actually ripping apart in my pubic bone area... felt like it was really going to collapse on me and I just put it down to the fact that it probably was. I don't know that I mentioned it a lot... I didn't say much to my doctor about anything. He was a doctor who just reassured you about things, said 'there! there!' sort of stuff... I may not have mentioned it to anyone.'*

Margaret remembered having several nightmares during this pregnancy:

> *'I'd come to in the middle of the night thinking the house was on fire and I'd be trying to get out...and then I'd come to and realize what I was doing and then I'd feel stupid.'*

She also remembered fainting:

> *'I did faint when I was pregnant...I've visions of coming to with David over me saying, 'You alright?' Might just have been with a tummy bug...used to do it anyway and I did do it when I was pregnant, but I don't remember the circumstances.'*

Margaret kept herself very busy during her pregnancy:

> *'I just worked and worked... longer than people normally did in those days. Most people who I knew who were pregnant, stopped working long before I did... I know people do that more now but I don't think they did then. It was about keeping me normal. I worked myself hard. I kept going. I didn't behave like a pregnant woman really. I*

*think really I behaved in many ways as though I wasn't pregnant...
but I don't remember saying to myself "I'm going to act as though
I'm not pregnant" but I think that's what I did.'*

Margaret remembered being excited about the fact she was going to have a
baby and being frightened about how she would cope with labour:

*'I was really scared I'd be out of control in the delivery - by that I
mean make a noise, fuss and be normal... the getting out of control
was about making a noise... and that's what I was afraid of - making
a noise... But in actual fact I didn't have time to do a lot of thinking
about things like that because I was working. Then, when I left work,
we shifted up to the North Island and at the stage, when most people
are preparing and feathering the nests and getting all ready to have
the baby, I was shifting house and going to a place where we didn't
know a soul...'*

David had a job in Masterton and he went on ahead three weeks
before Margaret. She worked until she was eight months pregnant and
then followed. They were moving on a Saturday into their new house
when Margaret went into labour three weeks early - *'lifted one packing
case too many!'*

Margaret had been to *'a couple of antenatal classes'* in Masterton and
had one antenatal check with the new doctor. She *'had done maternity,
delivering little babies. I knew what was meant to happen.'*

Birthing and Breast Feeding

Her waters broke at one a.m. on a Sunday morning. She remembered
feeling incredibly lonely, even though David was there. She felt a long way
from her mother and sister. She also remembered feeling scared,

*'Suddenly when I was in labour I thought, "Help, I can't turn it back
now .."'*

Margaret 'prepped' herself before she went into the maternity hospital. *'I
shaved myself before I went. I knew to do that...gave myself a short back and
sides...I knew so I did.'* She could not avoid the enema however:

*'The enema was awful, I didn't cope very well. Just the sensation of
the whole thing. I think it felt just so intrusive. I knew it was meant
to happen and I knew why they did it... I just self talked myself, well,
it had to be done. I found it very difficult. And I got up and had a
really good shower after it [laughs], which I don't think was
necessarily part of the routine... I just felt yuk!'*

Margaret was in labour from that Sunday morning until Tuesday
morning. Fifty six hours later, at eight thirty a.m., Jane was finally born:

*'I was having contractions frequently, but they weren't getting me
anywhere. It was ridiculous because she was only 6lb 4oz... It was*

uncomfortable... and it just went on and on... and on and on... All
I know is that I shouldn't have been left that long.'

At one stage Margaret was given an injection for pain relief. She hated that because she felt uncoordinated and out of control:

'That feeling a bit uncoordinated, that was really scary for me... I
wasn't in charge of me... it was bigger than I was sort of thing... it
was a loss of control and I really found that frightening.'

The baby was in a posterior position and Margaret's cervix was not dilating. Margaret described being too tired to be concerned:

'I just did my breathing and did what I had to do and got on with it.
I don't remember anyone being particularly concerned... I don't know
if I was too scared to let it happen - I don't know if you have that sort
of control over yourself or not. I think I was cooperative - I don't
remember causing any great problem in the sense of yelling or
screaming, tantrums or anything like that. I just fairly quietly got
on with what I had to do.'

Margaret did not remember seeing the doctor until some time on Monday evening when he suggested syntocinon spray to speed the process up. It was not common to leave women for so long in labour, but somehow Margaret was left alone, seemingly invisible, *'I just hid away in the room and most likely got forgotten about.'* She did not remember anyone examining her or listening to the foetal heart beat:

'I think I just curled up in the corner... in fact, thinking about it... I
was curled up right through my labour. I can see myself there now...
and I did, I just curled up... Curled up in a little ball and got on with
it.'

Margaret had her own room and David, who continued working, came and went as he could.

The main thing that Margaret could remember about the actual delivery was thinking, *'I've got to get it right..... Concentrating on my breathing and doing everything right...'* It was a relief for Margaret, the nurse, to be having her babies in Masterton not Christchurch, *'in case I misbehaved and the people I'd been tutoring would've been around.'* While Margaret felt some pressure to be a 'good patient', she did not remember wanting to scream:

'I guess I haven't been somebody who's yelled and screamed, in fact
that was what I found hardest... I couldn't make any sound, and I
think probably in actual fact, I think I made no noises. I think I was
just quiet... and I don't think I made any noise... Just got on and did
what I had to do without making any fuss or sound.'

For all her nursing training, Margaret was not worried at the time about the length of her labour:

'I wasn't analysing things as they went, which was interesting because I had to get it right... Had to get my breathing right, I'd practised long enough... I'd practised breathing. I had. So I must have thought about the birth...I used to practise breathing when my bowels moved, because I knew that when you panted, it relaxed all those muscles round there, so I practised then too... I hadn't thought about the delivery in the sense of actually what was going to happen, but I had thought about my breathing... I think it was all up this part of me that I thought about. I didn't think about down there. Yes, and that's where I concentrated - if I could keep that going then I'd be alright... Hey that's interesting, because that's actually what I did as a child. The things I practised were my breathing, and if I could keep breathing then he wouldn't kill me, because as long as I could keep breathing, I wouldn't suffocate... It was the breathing that I concentrated on and that's what I had to get right.'

And, obviously, that was what she did. She managed her whole long labour by breathing:

'It's true. It was a long time and I just kept quiet and I just did my breathing. I just got on with what I had to do and I breathed away every contraction. And then when it came to the second stage, when I actually wasn't allowed to push but wanted to, I panted away like mad... I got it right.'

This was really important for Margaret: *'I do remember being told, "Wow, you did well with your breathing!"'*

Margaret delivered on her back, hugging onto her legs. She remembered being *'shut up in myself. Particularly in theatre, I think I was just hiding down behind my knees really.'* It was painful, but Margaret had no pain relief. She refused the mask and she remembered pushing it away, *'No way, Jose,'* when they tried to administer it. She needed an episiotomy, which Margaret laughed about and felt was *'quite pathetic,'* given that her baby was quite small.

Although she felt no embarrassment or awareness of other people during the delivery, she recalled being acutely embarrassed afterwards:

'I was very embarrassed afterwards when they pan you and swab you down... I didn't like that at all and I got up and had a shower and washed my hair and got into trouble because you are not meant to do that after a long labour like mine.'

Margaret had a difficult time with Jane, who was a small baby and very jaundiced. Margaret was very lonely and although her sister and mother sent an enormous parcel containing ten little parcels, one to be opened each day, she missed them both terribly.

Breast feeding was problematic, the baby being jaundiced and sleepy.

Margaret had plenty of milk but very flat nipples, which meant it was hard for the baby to get onto the breast and Jane was tongue-tied. She was *'such a cute baby'* that the nurses would take her away and show her to other antenatal mothers *'in the hopes that that would spur them on.'* Margaret would get anxious about this and that also complicated feeding. After three weeks, Margaret, tired, lonely and stressed, decided to stop breastfeeding. She felt disappointed and a failure at stopping so early.

The baby suffered badly from colic until she was eight months old, then they learned she had a bowel obstruction. Jane cried all day, sometimes until nine or ten at night when she would finally fall asleep exhausted. At nine months, when Jane was due for an operation, the bowel spontaneously untwisted. Margaret herself was tense and exhausted but things began to improve from this time on.

Jane was twenty two months old when Ruth was born. Margaret was terrified that this baby might be as difficult as Jane. However, her pregnancy was good. Even the labour went well and Ruth was born within twenty four hours. Again, Margaret refused any pain relief *'I had to be in control.'* Margaret recalled that *'breathing was an issue to the extent it was important. I had to get it right again. I got it right.'* Again, Margaret made no sound. She remembered that she made

'no noise... too busy breathing. I certainly didn't make any fuss or noise... I just got on and did it... Even at the end I was aware what was going on, but I didn't make any noise.'

The emergency at the end of her labour, as she was delivering, was dramatic. The baby *'got stuck'* as her shoulders were bigger than her head. The doctor, with one foot on the bed and no time to lose, had to pull her out and Margaret's bladder was damaged. Margaret spoke in a cavalier way about this:

'It was O.K. Oh yeah it hurt. It certainly bruised my bladder badly. That was pretty painful. They were temporary things. There's no permanent damage...'

Again, Margaret had difficulty breast feeding. She fed Ruth briefly and enjoyed it more than with Jane. However, an abscess put a halt to her breast feeding within a few weeks. Margaret had conflicted feelings about breast feeding:

'Watching somebody else breast feeding in a relaxed happy way has got a nice feel about it... how it should be. For me it never quite felt like that. I don't think I was ever relaxed with it... the idea of it... I think it's lovely. When I was younger I was too embarrassed to see anyone else do it. I'd have been probably trying to hide it when I did it... It didn't come naturally and easily. The decision to bottle feed was a relief in practical terms. Sometimes I feel sad when I

think back.'

Margaret found everything much easier with this second child. She felt she bonded more easily with Ruth. But she described herself as a *'dreadfully over protective mother.'* She needed to know where her children were all the time and what was happening. In retrospect she thought she went *'a bit overboard.'*

Recovery

Five years ago, Margaret was prompted by several events to seek counselling. A casual conversation about the Homosexual Law Reform Bill, Margaret still didn't know what a homosexual was, and a passing question about sexual abuse brought on an extreme reaction in her body - she felt ill and her stomach *'went into knots.'* She began to have nightmares with similar themes - a child being killed, powerlessness or a face laughing. She would wake paralysed, unable to breathe. These were much worse if she and David had had intercourse. Also, David had a cancer scare and Margaret began to worry about her difficulties with sex. She felt guilty and sad. She thought she had *'short-changed'* David and feared, irrationally, that he might leave her.

Margaret knew she needed help. One morning, without knowing why she chose them, Margaret rang Rape Crisis. She met someone from that agency the same day who, after talking with her, suggested she talk with her doctor. Gathering all her courage, Margaret casually mentioned it to him at the beginning of the consultation and, fortunately, the doctor raised the topic again later. She was referred for counselling.

It was six months before Margaret began to remember her childhood. Small things, such as seeing a child do a handstand, hearing the wind blowing through trees or seeing a knife flashing, would trigger her memory and prompt a panic attack. She suffered panic attacks and nightmares, which intensified as new memories emerged. Margaret was unable to talk about anything. The counsellor commented to her on her inability to make any noise. Margaret began to write her memories down immediately after each session. Sometimes she would write for two hours before going home.

During some sessions, Margaret began to stop breathing and her counsellor organized another therapist to work alongside her:

'I have a strong memory - it came back through counselling... of this feeling with my breathing... things getting more and more distanced... a sort of noise in my ears and then just a blackness and a sort of drawing feeling as if I was speeding away - travelling - sucked along with the wind noise in my ears... almost like I was whizzing down this... being drawn down this blackness. Yet it wasn't frightening... and then I remember almost like a light, something warm

*at the end. Such a very vivid memory... one occasion particularly.
The way I recalled stuff was almost as if it was a replay - not with my
memory, with my body as if it was happening again.'*

At another point, triggered by a cancelled appointment, Margaret
became suicidal. She felt she was *'dragging everyone else down and it
wasn't fair'* to her husband and children to go on as she was. She had
organized a rope to hang herself and had just finished writing notes to her
family when David arrived home unexpectedly mid-morning.

Although it was difficult, Margaret remained working as a Practice Nurse
three days a week throughout these two years. It was important to her:

*'I coped by working there. I managed to switch out and get on with
the job. I was a nurse, I wasn't Margaret. I worked hard from nine
till six or seven in the evening, but that's how I had always coped
with things.'*

When Margaret began to remember, she was totally unable to have
sexual intercourse. Margaret and David took advice and did not try for
months. Then she and David *'started from scratch'* again - courting -
attempting to learn new patterns and arouse Margaret's sexuality. With
David's help, she gradually became desensitized to old triggers. She stated
that she can have sex in different positions now, can orgasm and enjoy it.
She can even initiate sex now, though mainly from her feelings for David,
rather than physical desire of her own; *'I start it often for him, but end up
enjoying it.'*

Ongoing Issues

Throughout the interviews, Margaret always referred to the man who
abused her as PKF. She felt a need to protect his family by shielding his
identity - he was, amongst other things, an elder of his church, a member of
the hospital board and was honoured for his services to the community. He
was, therefore, easily identifiable. However, although he was long dead,
Margaret also admitted that by always referring to him only by his initials
she managed to distance him,

*'Perhaps it is me not letting him be human... I think I prefer him not
to be a person.'*

Sex was a more enjoyable and intimate activity for Margaret now.
She no longer dreaded or avoided it. However, she did not naturally lubricate
and unless she consciously relaxed, penetration was still painful. Margaret
needed to use self talk, concentrate and make sure she remained present.
Breathing was still important:

*'I'm better than I was. That real freedom isn't there unless I make it.
If I consciously let myself go then I can freely enjoy it. But, actually,
I have to still tell myself.'*

Sometimes Margaret still experienced some discomfort during intercourse, which she was told was due to having a retroverted womb, a complication since childbirth. Margaret admitted that although corrective surgery would *'free her up'* even more, she was still *'not game enough to have the op. I battle with that. If I did then I could be much freer to enjoy.'* Margaret felt cheated and angry about what she and David had missed out on. She spoke of only being

'able to enjoy orgasm in the last two or three years. Bit short changed eh? Now we're getting older it's not as easy as it used to be... I get angry about that. We've been a bit pipped there... cheated... especially when in my job these kids come in who are sexually very active and often thoroughly enjoying themselves. It really makes me quite angry sometimes, that for us that wasn't the case for so many years. We've been married twenty five years this year, so we've been twenty two years without.'

Margaret expressed strong feelings of grief and loss in relation to her sexuality. This loss was mainly expressed in terms of what she has not been able to give David: *'I never did any giving sexually. It must have been awful for him.'* Although she knew it was irrational, she also tended to blame herself and feel guilty about this:

'I'm mad that the other's been spoiled for so long. Part of me feels quite guilty, although there's a sense in which it's inappropriate... it was beyond my being able to manage, but I do feel guilty about it... feel I cheated him for years and that makes me really sad, and then I get angry and then I think that's not going to get us anywhere.'

Margaret had a basically positive attitude to this, however. Speaking of being touched she said:

'I'm freed up in many ways now... Occasionally if caught off guard, I find myself flinching... a reflex reaction... occasionally... But it's good now. A late run is better than no run at all.'

Margaret's body remained a powerful reminder of her previous experiences. A number of times during the interviews she experienced strong sensations of discomfort. For example, when speaking of the conflicts she had as a child going to church and thinking that God lived in church and knew her secret, she looked very uncomfortable and said *'I can actually feel physical discomfort even now'*; when talking of Alan, *'even now thinking of it I feel quite "ick"...'* and talking about taking cervical smears:

'I really did have a physical reaction... I feel sick talking about it, isn't that interesting.'

Another noticeable physical response, still present, was hugging a cushion to herself when she began to speak of difficult experiences.

Throughout the interview, when she spoke of her sexuality, Margaret clutched a cushion to her stomach. Later, during the interview about her birthing experiences, she again picked up a cushion and hugged it to her stomach throughout.

Margaret also described the process she still used to manage difficult situations:

> *'Putting myself back together again for me involves shoving my feelings down out of the way and saying "O.K. get on with it, you've got things you've got to do, get on with them".'*

She made reference to using this process a number of times, for example, before the first interview when she had had bad news about a friend's poor cancer prognosis. While Margaret no longer totally suppressed her emotions, she could still effectively put them aside. She didn't cry for herself *'for thirty years'* and said that one of the hardest things for her in counselling was learning to cry. One way she *'shoved down'* her feelings was to be very busy. Margaret admitted that with David away, she was using *'busy-ness'* to cope, *'working flatstick all day'* then dropping asleep as soon as she stopped.

The most recent example Margaret had of the ongoing·effects of sexual abuse was in her work. As a Practice Nurse she was now required to do cervical smears. Just prior to our final interview she went on a training course for this. Performing smears has proven much more difficult than she anticipated:

> *'I've found, when I have a smear myself I can take myself away for a while, but I found it incredibly hard to do a smear on somebody else. I felt really intrusive and abusive doing it. I've really struggled with this. It actually stirred up a bit for me, because I couldn't switch out and do it. When I'm on the receiving end I can either psyche myself nowadays and go with it and cope with it because I've prepared myself, or, if I choose to, I can just take a little vacation while its happening. But I can't do that when I'm doing a smear on somebody else. I've actually got to concentrate on what I'm doing and I've got to be there. And I've found that really hard. In fact my sleep's gone all up the pole. While I was doing that course, I wasn't sleeping, hardly at all.'*

She also found herself eating large amounts of chocolate morsels, something she never usually did.

In the final interview, Margaret, looking back over her life, spoke of her relationships with other people:

> *'The closest relationships I've had are basically when I've been in a supportive role... they've been 'giving' relationships, if you know what I mean. I've been quite close to some people, but I*

haven't been the one doing the trusting... I've been the helper. So
I've met people quite closely, but it's been at their close level rather
than my close level... Even now, with David, although we're really
close, as I worked through the abuse and wrote my stuff, I let him
read it and talk about it if he wanted to. But that's the most. That's
pretty much David's style too.'

Of her other close relationship, with Mary her twin, she said, *'she*
would normally have been doing the talking.' Margaret spoke finally of
her loneliness:

'I was just thinking of the loneliness of my being abused and the
loneliness of my delivery in Masterton... I was just so lonely.'

The same loneliness was evident in her sexual experience, which lacked
mutuality and, like the other experiences was suffered quietly without telling
anyone, even David, her partner and closest companion.

This chapter has reported Margaret's life history in relation to her
abuse, her sexuality, her experiences of pregnancy and childbirth and finally
her recovery process. As much as possible, Margaret's own words have
been used to tell her story. In the following chapter her life history will be
analysed and discussed in relation to the perspectives that emerged in
reviewing the literature.

4
Analysis and Discussion

This chapter provides an analysis of Margaret's story as presented in the previous chapter, making links between the literature regarding childhood sexual abuse, sexuality and birthing and aspects of Margaret's own life history. The main focus is the examination of Margaret's intrapsychic experience and the influence of this on these key elements of her life. Other areas, such as her relationships with others and her career choice, are included where and as they contribute to her intrapsychic experience of these events.

Coping Strategies for the Childhood Abuse

Like any sexually abused child, Margaret survived by adaptation (Summit, 1983). To do this she developed a number of coping strategies and behaviours, which helped her survive while the abuse occurred and in her every day life throughout this time. The most important of these were her use of denial, dissociation and repression. These three coping strategies have recurred throughout her life and, in the case of the first two, seem to be on-going.

Denial

Denial appeared to have been Margaret's main adaptive response to the sexual abuse. Cornell and Olio (1991) defined denial as 'the defense patterns by which a person does not acknowledge portions of reality, dismissing them from conscious awareness in order to maintain an intrapsychic homeostasis' (p.61). Denial then can range from denial of the actual event, to denial of its importance. As Courtois (1988) described in relation to families, denial was an established pattern in Margaret's family for dealing with problematic issues. For example, her father's maintenance payments were kept secret. As the abuse occurred, Margaret denied its existence both to others, hiding tell-tale marks, remaining silent, and from herself, by her cleansing behaviour and chattering. As a child, Margaret also used reaction formation as a form of denial, to aid her efforts to remain silent and deny her experience. Her chattering about everything else but the trauma she was suffering indicated this. Later and for more than thirty years, she denied any memory of it.

Margaret successfully negotiated adolescence by denying herself any awareness of her own sexuality or sexuality in general. This withdrawal response is described in the literature (Courtois, 1988; Maltz & Holman, 1987) and reflected Margaret's fears, negative self image and avoidance of developing a sexual identity. Margaret only allowed herself friendship relationships with males and did not acknowledge the possibility of any sexual relationship. Alan, the one persistent male who threatened that position, was feared and shunned. That Margaret managed to navigate training and work in nursing without gaining any knowledge of sexual behaviour and things sexual, seems incredible. Obviously, however, she did. At forty two Margaret had no understanding of what being homosexual meant. Those instances she remembered in her nursing career where sexuality became dangerously close to awareness, were dealt with by avoidance and by maintaining silence, a response discussed in the literature. (Cornell & Olio, 1991; Courtois, 1991)

Denial of any sexual feelings was also an established pattern throughout her courtship with David, possibly reinforced by their Christian beliefs. This, and the physical distance resulting from it, allowed Margaret the safety of developing a relationship with a man. However, Margaret's denial of her own sexuality appeared to have become increasingly entrenched as she approached marriage, with no thought of physical intimacy or sex.

From the beginning of her marriage, Margaret experienced considerable sexual difficulties with arousal, performance and satisfaction. Such difficulties have been commonly reported in the literature (Deighton & McPeek, 1985; Jehu, 1988; McGuire & Wagner, 1978). Even after the disastrous attempts at sex on her honeymoon, Margaret denied to herself and to David the extent and importance of her difficulties.

Silence seemed to have played a major part in the maintenance of denial. Margaret appeared to have remained totally silent about her difficulties with sex and her experiences during her first birth. As is commonly the case (Finkelhor, 1983; Summit, 1983), Margaret as a child told no one of the sexual abuse to which she was subjected. While no connection is made in the literature, it is possible that the silence around these three experiences (abuse, sexual activity and birthing), described more fully below, is connected and may be grounded in the childhood sexual abuse experience

Margaret told no one of the difficulties she experienced around sex. Although at some level Margaret must have registered difficulty, as she and David experimented with different positions until they found two that allowed penetration, she never queried this with anyone, not even David. As a nurse she knew when to use a lubricant. However, she and David did not acknowledge and discuss these matters together. This seemed at odds with their otherwise close communication and caring. The non-communication about sex mirrored Margaret's lack of communication as a child with both her mother and her sister. Although their relationship was close and caring, they were told nothing of Margaret's abuse. She remained silent, just as she remained silent about her difficulties with sex. Margaret appeared to have both minimized and denied the sexual difficulties, using a familiar path of silent resignation.

Margaret had been threatened with not making a sound as a child and this injunction seemed also to have operated strongly when Margaret gave birth to Jane. Courtois (1988) commented on injunctions learned during childhood sexual abuse that continued into adulthood and caused survivors to disregard their body states and their needs. Although Margaret laboured for fifty six hours, she did so with almost no intervention and she was exceptionally quiet. She asked for nothing and received nothing. Her lack of sound appeared in this instance to have helped make her invisible.

It seemed extraordinary that Margaret should have been left alone for so long while in labour. She had a fear of *'making a fuss,'* but her soundless invisibility possibly arose from a much deeper ingrained response pattern. It is even more extraordinary that Margaret, herself a nurse experienced in delivery, did not register any distress around the length of her labour. She did not remember any concern and appeared to have denied to herself that her labour was overly long or in any way complicated. Here again, as suggested by the literature (Cornell & Olio, 1991) she appeared to both deny the experience as it occurred and denied its importance. Her denial to herself, as in her denial around sexuality and also in her childhood abuse experience, seemed to have been so strong that other people registered no concern and, therefore, correspondingly showed none.

Margaret's use of writing seemed also to be an adaptive responsive to the silence forced on her as a child. The importance writing can play in the therapy of sexual abuse survivors is well documented (Bass & Davis, 1988). Certainly for Margaret, writing became an important part of communicating with intimacy, as can be seen in the development of the relationship with David and also in her communication of her abuse as she worked through it during the recovery process. Writing may have been Margaret's way of expressing herself safely without making a sound.

In all three nodal experiences, the abuse, sexual activity and birth, Margaret used cleansing behaviour, which possibly helped her deny the existence of the experience after the event. After being abused she was told to wash in the river and she reported spending much time in the bathroom after her return home. After sex she would always jump up and have a *'good wash,'* which meant David was asleep on her return. During her labour, after the *'invasive'* enema, Margaret had a *'good shower.'* After the birth, although weak and risking breaking the rules, Margaret dragged herself off to the shower. Washing and showering seemed to be an almost ritualistic way of denying each experience and ridding herself of the feelings each stirred up.

Denial, therefore, was a coping strategy Margaret developed in childhood. As a result of the sexual abuse she experienced, she learned to deny both an experience as it happened and its significance in her life. In the three areas under study, Margaret did this by not communicating with others, by using cleansing behaviour and by not allowing herself the reality of her experience. As posited in the literature (Cornell & Olio, 1991), this denial increased in tenacity as it combined with dissociation, another coping strategy developed in childhood and central to Margaret's attempts to deal with the long-term effects of childhood sexual abuse.

Dissociation.

Margaret developed a number of ways of dissociating from her body in order to manage overwhelming feelings. In a dissociative state, affect and emotional significance are unconsciously split off from, for example, a situation or a relationship (Cornell & Olio, 1991). This response is a common coping strategy developed by sexual abuse survivors (Cornell & Olio, 1991; Courtois, 1988; Sheldrick, 1991).

·It seemed Margaret developed two ways of dissociating, both of which were linked to her breathing, which she regarded as a key to her survival. She practised breathing with determination as a child and learned to control herself by using it. She also learned to stop breathing and lose consciousness, or 'faint', when things became too difficult. As a child she used both of these options. She practised breathing in bed at night, presumably for use when she felt suffocated and overwhelmed. When the abuse was too intense, she stopped breathing and presumably fainted, thereby removing herself from the horror of the experience.

Margaret reported fainting frequently when she was young. This was associated with menstruating and occurred also during sexual activity when she was newly married. Both situations appeared to relate to painful experiences. She also remembered fainting during pregnancy, and this may have been associated with pain or it may have had an alternative physiological explanation such as diarrhoea. Margaret did describe unusual painful feelings of being *'ripped apart'* in her pubic bone area which may have prompted a fainting response. Certainly her extreme reactions to menstrual pain and sexual activity were possibly due to the associations they stirred, because of their physical affinity with the early sexual abuse. Fainting, therefore, appeared to be a major break of consciousness and the body's response to pain associated with the original trauma.

Breathing, on the other hand, was Margaret's way of staying in control without losing consciousness. It is likely, however, that Margaret used this also to achieve a dissociated state. Cornell and Olio (1991) described this state as a more subtle and persistent loss of contact with others. During the long hours of her labour, Margaret used the same technique with breathing she had pactised as a child to survive. It was, for her, *'the most important thing,'* and she *'had to get it right.'* Her determination to remain in control through breathing seemed enormous and totally absorbing. She also seemed to have used breathing to *'split off'* the lower part of her body from the top. She concentrated on her breathing and was thereby able to dissociate from the painful feelings and sensations she was experiencing during labour. This same concentrated breathing may also have dissociated her from contact with others, which meant she was invisible and left alone.

Margaret used dissociation during sex to *'space herself'* out. This is a common technique used by sexual abuse survivors to manage sexual activity (Bergart, 1986; Courtois, 1991; Deighton & McPeek, 1986; Gordy, 1983; Sheldrick, 1991). Margaret disconnected her mind from the physical experience, and focused on trivia, ignoring sensations and the experience of her body. She still needed to breathe consciously to relax, in order to allow painless penetration, and concentrated on combating her former dissociative pattern by self-talking to stay present. Though much better, this still required conscious effort.

Controlling breathing and not breathing has, therefore, been an important part of Margaret's coping strategies. These two behaviours were the means by which Margaret initially managed the sexual abuse trauma and later her sexual and birthing experiences. The techniques she developed as a child she carried over unconsciously into these other areas, as throughout all of this time Margaret had no conscious memory of the original trauma because she had so effectively repressed this.

Repression.

Margaret has very few childhood memories prior to the abuse stopping. It seems, as the literature suggested (Browne & Finkelhor, 1986; Courtois, 1991; Herman & Schatzow, 1987), that due to the seriousness of the abuse, caused by her young age at onset, the sadism and violence that accompanied it and the age of the perpetrator, Margaret repressed all memory of it. Certainly her amnesia about the sexual abuse and much of her childhood was pervasive, and resulted in a major loss of personal history (Cornell & Olio, 1991) still only partially restored.

This repression, however, possibly enabled Margaret to function successfully throughout a large part of her life. The few times when it appeared to have failed, were when Margaret was caught off guard and confronted with some aspect of male sexuality for which she was unprepared. This occurred when Margaret as a nurse was exposed to events that resembled the abuse. It seemed that the impact of each occurrence was more severe than the last, with the event in Masterton causing a major disturbance in Margaret's body's functioning beyond her control or awareness.

Courtois (1991) suggested that normal developmental events like birthing and death can trigger memories. In Margaret's case, it seemed these memories were triggered at a physical, somatic and emotional level and activated the appropriate coping strategies to manage them and keep them from awareness. It was Margaret's life stage, her awareness of her husband's mortality and fear of desertion, which finally allowed her repression to lessen and her memories to emerge. The repression disappeared little by little in therapy as issues began to be addressed and familiar things, for example wind blowing through trees and a child doing a handstand, became significant triggers for her.

The return in therapy of Margaret's somatic symptoms as the amnesia dispersed, was significant in that it suggested that her body held and stored memories that it could activate without conscious awareness. Courtois (1991), discussing the process of memory retrieval, outlined the variety of ways sexual abuse survivors' memories can return. She commented that remembering can occur emotionally, physiologically - 'through body memories and perceptions,' somatically - 'through pain, illness (often without medical diagnosis), nausea and conversion symptoms such as paralysis and numbing,' and, 'that the body may react in pain reminiscent of the abuse.' (p.26) Although there is no direct connection made in the literature, it seems likely that Margaret's repression was also significantly tested in sexual encounters and her birthing experiences, especially the first, because these were intense body experiences. Her extensive use of both denial and dissociation to manage these experiences suggests that the sensate experience of her body was pushing at the repression of memory. Certainly the sexual assault experience, when she was nursing at Masterton, which occurred after she had given birth, produced a much more dramatic physical response. Her body was perhaps becoming increasingly difficult to ignore.

Margaret's use of repression, therefore, enabled the memory of the sexual trauma she suffered as a child to remain out of her consciousness and this allowed her to function successfully in many areas of her life. There were times when this was tested and these involved physical experiences and caused somatic reactions. Birthing and sexuality, like sexual abuse, are physical experiences that are intense, potentially overwhelming and involve the same areas of, and sensations in, the body. During her sexual and birthing experiences, Margaret's ability to keep the memory of the abuse experience out of awareness, was, therefore, more difficult and resulted in an intensification of her use of denial and dissociation.

Physical and Somatic Consequences of the Coping Strategies

Margaret, like other survivors (Courtois, 1988) was adept at minimizing or disregarding her physical experience and bodily needs. As identified in the literature (Bachmann, et al., 1988; Courtois, 1988; Harrop Griffeths, et al., 1988; Walker, et al., 1988), Margaret experienced chronic pelvic pain. This was associated with menstruation, when it was so intense she frequently fainted, with sexual activity when she experienced *'a real dragging ache for several days after,'* and during pregnancy when it felt like she *'was ripping apart in [her] pubic bone area.'*

Margaret, however, did not consult a doctor or even query the reason for this pain, but seemed to have unquestioningly accepted it. This kind of response is noted in the literature (Bachmann, et al., 1988; Courtois, 1988). Margaret had, and has still, a marked difficulty with any surgical or gynaecological procedures performed on herself, although as a nurse she was familiar with medical procedures. She dealt with this, like other survivors (Courtois, 1988), by avoidance or minimizing the importance of the problem. She either denied the importance of its existence or was reluctant to consult the doctor.

Margaret's response to physical pain was to go off alone and curl up in a foetal position, hugging herself until it passed. She did this in the back yard shed with her toy dog on her return home from the 'picnics', as a teenager and a nurse with severe menstrual pain, and when she gave birth to Jane; both in labour and delivery she *'curled up in a little ball and got on with it.'* One of her two possible intercourse positions involved hugging a pillow to her stomach and at difficult moments in our interviews, she took a pillow and hugged it to herself throughout. It seemed that not only did her body unconsciously remember the pain, it also unconsciously, through well worn patterns, attended to it.

Margaret's other ingrained pattern, developed also as a child, was her 'busy-ness.' Over functioning, hyper-alertness and hyper-vigilance are all reported in the literature (Courtois, 1988). Margaret's 'busy-ness' emerged in childhood, primarily through sport, where she managed to protect herself from the abuse by over involvement elsewhere. This was one way she obtained some control. Sporting activity was maintained into early adulthood, where it was replaced by hard work on her nursing course. She possibly kept sexual activity to a minimum through her marriage by working herself until she was exhausted. When she was pregnant Margaret worked much longer than was normal at the time. At the end of her term, she was able to be totally preoccupied with moving to a new town and house. Even there she did not slow down, but set off her labour three weeks early by lifting one packing case too many. 'Busy-ness' seems to have been a learned response that enabled her to manage anxiety in a way that was acceptable to her.

This over-functioning appeared to have enabled Margaret to manage her life and achieve some control over her unconscious processes. She also learned to avoid semi-conscious states, where repressed memories might escape into awareness. She had difficulty going to sleep as a child until she had learned to control semi-consciousness with dreams of rescuing. As a teenager, she studied late into the night. In later life, she worked *'until she dropped'*, thereby avoiding semi-consciousness when repressed memories might have emerged.

Margaret also suffered considerable sleep disturbances, another long-term consequential symptom noted in the literature (Finkelhor & Browne, 1986; Sheldrick, 1991). She had nightmares that occurred as a child, after sexual activity when she was first married, when pregnant and during her recovery process. While Margaret's conscious mind could control her responses and deny her experience, her unconscious mind was beyond this control. Over these times when the connections among these four experiences were so marked, her unconscious mind reacted strongly. This response still occurs; Margaret's sleep pattern *'went all up the pole'* at the time of our final interview when she was experiencing difficulties performing cervical smears.

In summary, because of the childhood sexual abuse she was subjected to, Margaret suffered both a number of physical and somatic consequences, and developed ways of dealing with these that are common in sexual abuse survivors. Both the consequences and Margaret's ways of dealing with them emerged and intensified after sexual activity, during pregnancy and labour, and through her recovery process.

Consequences for Social Functioning and Interpersonal Relationships

One positive outcome of Margaret's 'busy-ness' was the success she achieved in her activities. Although not *'naturally sporty'*, she represented her province in indoor basketball, graduated with highest marks in her nursing year and was the youngest nursing tutor the teaching hospital had ever appointed. Such successes by sexual abuse survivors are noted in the literature (Brunngraber, 1986; Courtois, 1988; Gordy, 1983), where they are attributed to positive qualities developing out of the abuse experience. While this is possibly applicable to Margaret, her success also resulted from the nature of this particular coping strategy of keeping busy.

Success, however, was at the expense of Margaret caring for herself both physically and emotionally. This dynamic is described in the literature (Courtois, 1988; Herman & Schatzow, 1987). As previously mentioned, Margaret tended to disregard and minimize any bodily pain and, until her recovery, her emotional life was impaired. She denied her feelings, not crying for herself for example *'for thirty years'*. Her life lacked intimacy. Physical intimacy and emotional closeness in her sexual life were severely restricted. Emotional intimacy also seemed to have been lacking in other relationships. In caring for others before herself, Margaret placed herself in the rescuing role with most of her friends. She was unable to share herself with them. She listened but did not confide. Similarly with her closest relationships, her sister and her husband, they mostly did the talking and, while she cared deeply for them, she seemed to have been unable to share herself intimately with them.

Margaret wanted to be a nurse from an early age. Courtois (1988) has drawn attention to the lack of research on the effects of childhood sexual abuse on later career development and functioning. Margaret's choice of career is revealing. While she had some learning difficulties, which she attributed to the sexual abuse she had endured, as a teenager and during her nursing training she resourcefully found ways of overcoming these and turned them to her advantage. Such self reliance and autonomy reinforces Brunngraber's (1986) hypothesis that those qualities developed in childhood to deal with the sexual abuse, serve some survivors well in adult life.

Nursing offered Margaret the opportunity to fulfil the desire she had identified in childhood - to care for sick people. The choice is interesting in the light of her lack of care for herself and the imbalance in her relationships, previously noted, between her disregard for her own needs and her sensitivity to those of others. Her choice of career allowed her legitimate 'rescuing' of other people and denial of herself.

Being a nurse also meant that Margaret could develop an understanding of bodies without having a close relationship with her own. It provided her with a clinical distance from herself. She could differentiate menstrual cramps from appendicitis, was aware that KY jelly was a useful lubricant, knew to shave herself before going to hospital, what happened in delivery and why she needed an enema. It was as if nursing enabled her to manage her body's needs without having to understand them. Margaret never asked herself why, because she did not want to know, and being a nurse meant she did not need to. She could manage.

Being a nurse may also have meant that she could unconsciously project those 'sick' parts of herself outwards, where she could care for them in a way that was acceptable to her. She had a perfect opportunity to remain cut off from herself and her bodily needs, and at the same time to look after herself in the healthiest way possible for her at the time.

Margaret's nursing experience helped her to negotiate hospital procedures during birthing better than many women. The literature suggested that these procedures were serious obstacles to women having positive subjective experiences of childbirth (Kitzinger, 1983; Leifer, 1980; Oakley, 1980; Raphael-Leff, 1980; Young, 1984). Because Margaret was familiar with hospitals and had been a part of such institutions for a number of years, she was perhaps less alienated and more accepting of the routines. She still found these procedures invasive, however, and avoided them where she could.

Margaret was compliant and non-judgmental about her experiences with doctors at this time, a common response noted by Courtois (1988) and attributed by Young (1984) to feelings of alienation. She never displayed critical or bitter feelings concerning doctors' sometimes inadequate interventions. She tended to blame herself and her body's idiosyncrasies rather than question the level of expertise she had received.

Possibly because she was a nurse, Margaret managed her feelings of alienation, as identified in the literature (Young, 1984), better than others. She probably shared medical staffs' assumptions and goals. Contrary to many women's experience, she maintained a large degree of autonomy and control over her birth process. She experienced a marked lack of intervention, possibly because she was already compliant and passive and did not require 'controlling', but also because she created no fuss, was 'in control' and was, therefore, left to herself. Margaret's ability to use breathing to dissociate enabled her to maintain control, just as her denial prevented her from becoming alarmed.

Margaret's need to control her birth process appears to be a marrying of the expectations and skills learned by being a nurse and her need to stay in control. She was determined to *'get it right'* and not disgrace herself, and equally not to pass over any control to nursing staff by requiring medication. It seemed she might have extended her nursing skills to herself, and managed to 'nurse' herself through fifty six hours of labour.

To summarize, the effects of childhood sexual abuse were evident in Margaret's achievements in her career, her social functioning and her interpersonal relationships. Her choice of career was possibly linked to her childhood experience, and nursing also helped her address later issues in her life arising from the abuse. Despite these positive outcomes, Margaret tended to disregard herself and her own needs and her capacity for intimacy was impaired.

Emotional Consequences and Self-Perceptions

Margaret shared emotional responses common to survivors. However, depression, the most common long-term effect (Browne & Finkelhor, 1986), did not feature in her experience. Similarly, self destructive behaviour, another noted behaviour in sexual abuse survivors (Browne & Finkelhor, 1986; Courtois, 1988), did not extend beyond her readiness to place others' needs before her own and her over-functioning as previously discussed.

Busy activity appeared to compensate for an underlying sense of powerlessness, which may have contributed to high levels of generalized anxiety manifested through sleep disturbance and tension. This dynamic was widely discussed in the literature (Briere & Runtz, 1989; Browne & Finkelhor, 1986; Courtois, 1988; Sheldrick, 1991). Margaret seemed to have experienced higher levels of generalized anxiety when she was pregnant. As pregnancy requires increased attention to the self and increased consciousness of one's body (Offerman-Zuckerberg, 1980; Raphael-Leff, 1980; Young, 1984), it seems likely that Margaret, who paid so little attention to either, may have experienced increased internal conflict. This was possibly expressed physically in the symptoms outlined by Offerman-Zuckerberg (1980), such as excessive nausea, unspecific pain and cramps in the genital area, fainting and digestive upsets, and also through the nightmares, fainting and hyper-activity she described.

Margaret managed anxiety in a number of ways. Her nightmares may be regarded as an attempt to manage aroused anxiety. She also resorted to eating sweets. While this did not constitute an eating disorder, as discussed by Lobel (1991) and Oppenheimer (1985), this pattern did seem to have been set in place in childhood. Eating the bags of lollies she was brought was one way of dispelling the horror of her experience. When she was pregnant, Margaret must have eaten considerable amounts of sugar to have developed such high levels in her urine. She also reported an increased sugar intake when learning to do the stressful cervical smear tests.

Margaret's high sugar levels when she was pregnant with Jane, therefore, possibly indicated a high level of anxiety. This supports Jacobs' (1991) suggestion that pregnancy activates increased anxiety and underlying eating disorders in sexual abuse survivors. In Romanik's (1982) sample, pregnancy also created increased anxiety, with each of his subjects reporting associated fear as children of becoming pregnant to their abusers. That sexual abuse survivors should suffer increased anxiety during pregnancy for these and other reasons seems highly likely.

Another indication of a marked increase in Margaret's anxiety during pregnancy and labour, was the increased presence of her coping strategies. Coping strategies are formed as a response to trauma and stress, therefore it seems likely that their increased use could indicate some resurgence of the originating anxiety. When she was pregnant, Margaret experienced somatic pain, her pelvic bone felt like it was *'ripping apart'*, her nightmares recurred and she used considerable denial, working herself *'extremely hard.'* Margaret 'handled' her long labour by using dissociation to control her breathing.

This anxiety possibly had a marked impact on the course and duration of Margaret's labour. The relationship between maternal anxiety and pre-term and obstetric difficulties during labour (Georgas, et al., 1984; Gorsuch & Key, 1974; Jones, 1978) and length of labour (Jacobs 1991; Lederman, et al., 1979) has been well documented. Margaret herself had no explanation for her long labour. Jane was a relatively small baby and Margaret's pelvis was not small. It was *'just a difficult first birth.'* As previously discussed, Margaret, as a nurse herself, was unlikely to have been deeply affected by alienation from the hospital setting.

Anxiety, therefore, may have triggered her body's memory response which interfered with the natural flow of labour. Boadella (1987) contended that tension patterns are held in the body and 'can be looked on as a person's frozen history.' (p.7) If the body remembers sensations and pain, and reacts accordingly, Margaret's body, rather than allowing the baby's birth, may have reacted against it, thereby prolonging her labour. That Margaret did not have such a difficult experience with her second birth may support this notion. The second birth would draw more heavily on Margaret's first birth experience, which she managed successfully eventually.

The body may be viewed as holding memories of pain and fear sensations from the trauma of childhood sexual abuse. If flashbacks can cause a recurrence of physical sensations, such as pain or nausea, or a physiological response as described by Courtois (1991), and sexual activity can also prompt this response (Jehu, 1988; Maltz & Holman, 1987), then it is likely that the same process is triggered during the birth process. The physical, fundamental and overwhelming nature of birth may then have triggered body responses in Margaret that had long been repressed. The resulting increased fear and tension may have interfered with the normal process of her labour. Boadella (1987) described the physiological effects of anxiety on women in labour and contended that it was likely to both prolong the experience and render it more painful.

The sexual nature of childbirth also possibly complicated Margaret's response to labour and helped prolong it. Undrugged birth can be a sexual experience (Kitzinger, 1983; Newton, 1979), therefore Margaret was trapped in a dilemma. She feared losing control and so refused pain relief, leaving herself fully conscious throughout. However, she was equally unable to allow herself to be overwhelmed by a potentially sexual experience. Her only option was to struggle unwittingly against the physical sensations, using breathing as a dissociative technique to maintain this, with her very long labour as the result .

Margaret's experience with breast feeding also raised the possibility that for sexual abuse survivors breast feeding may be fraught with added difficulties. While no literature was located specifically on this subject, breastfeeding has also been described as a sexual experience by Kitzinger (1983) and Newton (1979). If a woman is uneasy about her sexuality and breast feeding is a sexual experience, then the likelihood of difficulties with feeding may increase. Difficulties with breast feeding can also be a consequence of difficult births (Kitzinger 1979), which sexual abuse survivors may be more likely to experience.

Margaret's tendency to blame herself, accept responsibility and feel guilty is a common reaction noted in the literature (Bergart, 1986; Deighton & McPeek, 1985; Frawley & McInerney, 1987; Gordy, 1983). Margaret still felt guilty about her treatment of Alan, the first boy who showed real interest in her, and she had a deep sense of guilt and loss in relation to her sexual life with David. Her difficulty menstruating she saw as being *'just her'* and she described taking so long to deliver a six pound baby as *'ridiculous'*. Her tendency to accept responsibility personally and blame herself was deep-seated.

The predominant feeling Margaret remembered and spoke of during our interviews was extreme loneliness. Feelings of loneliness, isolation and alienation are often experienced by sexual abuse survivors (Bergart, 1986; Blake, White & Kline, 1985; Browne & Finkelhor, 1986; Gordy, 1983; Sheldrick, 1991). As a child, during sexual activity, during labour and post-natally, Margaret's loneliness was profound. Along with her inability to make a sound and her concentration on her breathing, loneliness seems to dominate her experience in the areas specifically under study.

The aim of this research was to explore the potential relationship between childhood sexual abuse, and sexuality, pregnancy and birthing. This chapter presented these as nodal points in Margaret's life. Her experiences of these were highlighted, connections and links among them made, and her story analysed and related to the literature previously reviewed. Some hypotheses and possible theories that arise from these connections will be discussed in the last chapter.

5
Summary, Conclusion and Further Considerations

One of the valuable contributions in-depth case research has to offer is its capacity to generate theory and hypotheses (Faraday & Plummer, 1979). This study has generated a number of hypotheses which will be outlined here, as will conclusions that can be drawn from them. Further consideration of these in relation to obstetric and gynaecological care will be suggested and suggestions for future research in this area made.

Summary

Margaret's experience of childhood sexual abuse had a major impact on her life. She learned to minimize her physical experience, rely only on herself for support and comfort when under great duress, and over-function as a way of managing her life. The qualities this developed helped her function very successfully, especially in her choice of career. However, these same responses restricted her capacity for intimacy and possibly increased her sense of loneliness and isolation.

The three major coping strategies Margaret developed to deal with the childhood bodily trauma - denial, dissociation and repression - were both useful and unhelpful. Denial enabled Margaret to function, but at the same time she was denied the reality of her experience and therefore remained trapped within it. Similarly, the two methods of dissociation Margaret developed and used in conjunction with this denial, controlled breathing and not breathing, helped her maintain control by disintegrating her experience. At the same time it meant she was distanced both from herself (her awareness of her own experience) and from others. Repression kept the memory of childhood sexual abuse from her awareness, allowing her to function successfully, but this was at the expense of her physical well-being. Margaret had to work extremely hard to avoid semi-consciousness and still at times she was physically affected by a number of somatic reactions. These three coping strategies came under considerable pressure, and increased markedly around events concerning sexuality, pregnancy and birthing.

Conclusions

For a number of reasons the results of this research suggest a relationship between childhood sexual abuse and birthing. Margaret experienced an intensifying of the coping strategies she developed as a child, when she became involved in sexual activity and as she approached giving birth. Margaret used denial and dissocation to cope with sexuality and sexual experience. While she was pregnant, nightmares and denial played a major role, and during her labour her control of her breathing, her lack of sound and her aloneness formed a major part of her experience. The coping strategies developed originally to enable emotional survival, came once more to the fore.

While many women experience fear and tension around childbirth, sexual abuse survivors may experience considerable additional stress. This is not only because both experiences are closely linked physically, especially given current hospital routines, but also because of the psychological pain that accompanies the physical response. Margaret's coping strategies appeared to intensify as she approached delivery; her breathing, her aloneness and her silence are significant indicators of anxiety and fear. Margaret did not discuss pain, her experience seemed to have been dominated by her previous response to physical trauma - a childhood determination to survive by breathing.

It appeared then that the domains of abuse, sexuality, pregnancy and birthing were linked somatically. Each experience involved to some extent similar body parts, sensate focus and physiological responses. The intimate nature of each experience, the cultural taboos that surround each one and the lowering or invasion of body boundaries, meant that emotional as well as somatic responses in each situation could be linked. Coping strategies that developed in response to the original trauma provide the connection between the experience of childhood sexual abuse and later experiences of sexuality, pregnancy and birthing. These strategies may have been used unconsciously again, possibly assuming a different form or increased intensity because of the somatic and emotional links that exist among the related experiences.

Two possibilities were previously stated:

(i) that sexual abuse survivors' pregnancies may be more conflicted due to the similar nature of the emotional and somatic effects that both pregnancy and sexual abuse elicit; and

(ii) that these symptoms in pregnancy themselves arouse memories of sexual abuse and, therefore, increase internal conflicts during pregnancy for sexual abuse survivors.

Margaret's experience supports these possibilities. She did not appear to experience the psychological disturbances Offerman-Zuckerberg

(1980) noted among pregnant women, such as depression and self destructiveness, which could have been due to the pattern of denial she had formed. She did, however, experience almost all of the physical symptoms Offerman-Zuckerberg (1980) listed, such as fainting and breathing difficulties, and this is possibly due to her having less control over these.

Margaret's physical symptoms also support Offerman-Zuckerberg's (1980) conclusions that, where a discrepancy between conscious and unconscious attitudes exists, and this was the case for Margaret due to the repressed material she was carrying, somatic symptoms are more frequent and anxiety is much higher. These same physical symptoms possibly triggered her 'maintain control by being busy' response, and began the process of arousing in her body memories of the abuse, thereby increasing internal conflict.

High anxiety appeared to have been a major factor in Margaret's first birthing experience. The length of her labour supports Jacobs' (1991) hypothesis, as does her high level of anxiety indicated by her high sugar intake and increased activity. These factors endorse Romanik's (1982) suggestion that pregnancy may present specific stress for childhood sexual abuse survivors.

Further Considerations

Margaret's story suggests a relationship between the experiences of sexual abuse, and sexuality, pregnancy and birthing, especially a first birth. The results reinforce clinical understandings of the difficulties sexual abuse survivors may experience in dealing with ordinary gynaecological issues and problems. They also suggest that sexual abuse survivors may have increased difficulty with breast feeding due to its sexual nature. The link between birthing difficulties and subsequent difficulties with breast feeding and bonding, is well established (Kitzinger, 1979). If sexual abuse survivors are more likely to suffer a difficult first birth, then breast feeding and bonding are likely also to be problematic.

These possibilities raise a number of questions and issues regarding gynaecological, antenatal, perinatal and postnatal care of sexual abuse survivors. For example, difficulties relating to menstruation need further research and clarification. Also, invasive procedures, however seemingly simple, need to be reappraised in the light of the links explored here. The increased stress they potentially present for sexual abuse survivors needs to be recognized. Similarly, early identification of women at risk in this way could eliminate unnecessary difficulties for both mothers and babies.

The relationship between childhood sexual abuse and later birthing experience and the implications of this require considerable further study. The exploratory findings here in relation to a single life history deserve to be pursued in larger studies using a number of subjects. The issue of repression, however, complicates the area. If, as the literature suggests (Courtois, 1991; Lundberg-Love, et al., 1991), up to 50% of survivors do not recall being abused, then identifying those who have been abused will always be problematic and studies using community samples and control groups need careful sample selection. It is impossible to define how different Margaret's experience of her sexuality or of birthing would have been if she had remembered the abuse that she had suffered. Comparisons also need to be investigated between those who were sexually abused and had undergone recovery work before giving birth, and those who had not done so. In addition, it is important that the signs that indicate childhood sexual abuse continue to be researched and collated. Certainly suggestions for screening and attempts to screen for sexual abuse in psychiatric referrals (Lundberg-Love, 1991; Mullen, et al., 1988) are positive steps that need to be extended to other patient populations.

Women's responses to childhood sexual abuse are, on investigation, understandable and sensible reactions to traumatic situations. The long-term ramifications of these responses, however, can be detrimental. Further research is required and findings need to be disseminated if women sexually abused in childhood are to be assisted to maximize their opportunities to recover and to experience later developmental stages in their lives without constrictions imposed by the earlier trauma. Margaret's story is witness to the strength, courage and tenacity in one such life. As she herself commented, in relation to the changes which emerged from her own recovery process,

'A late run is better than no run at all!'

References

Armstrong, N. (1991). Research methods in womens studies: Study Guide Two. Palmerston North: Massey University.

Bachmann, G.A., Moeller, T.P., & Benett, J. (1988). Childhood sexual abuse and the consequences in adult women. American Journal of Obstetrics and Gynaecology, 71(4), 631-642.

Bass, E. & Davis, L. (1988). The courage to heal: a guide for women survivors of child sexual abuse. New York: Harper & Row.

Benedek, T. (1970). The psychobiology of pregnancy. In E.J. Anthony & T. Benedek (Eds.), Parenthood: its psychology and psychopathology. Boston: Little Brown.

Benward, J. & Denson-Gerber, J. (1975). Incest as a causative factor in anti-social behaviour: an exploratory study. Contemporary Drug Problems, 4 (3), 323-340.

Bergart, A.M. (1986). Isolation to intimacy: incest survivors in group therapy. Social Casework: The Journal Contemporary Social Work, 66 (7), 266-275.

Bibring, G. (1961). Some considerations of the psychological process in pregnancy. The Psychoanalytical Study of the Child, 14, 113-121.

Blake-White, J. & Kline, C.M. (1985). Treating the dissociative process in adult victims of childhood incest. Social Casework: The Journal of Contemporary Social Work, 66 (7), 394-403.

Blum, B.L. (Ed.). (1980). Psychological aspects of pregnancy, birthing and bonding. New York: Human Sciences Press.

Boadella, D. (1987). Life streams: an introduction to biosynthesis. London: Routledge & Kegan Paul.

Brannen, J. (1988). Research note: the study of sensitive subjects. Sociological Review, 36 (3), 552-563.

Briere, J. & Runtz, M. (1988). Symptomatology associated with childhood sexual victimization in a non-clinical adult sample. Child Abuse & Neglect, 12, 51-59.

Briere, J. & Runtz, M. (1989). Post sexual abuse trauma. In J. Briere (Ed.), Therapy for adults molested as children: beyond survival (pp. 85-99). New York: Springer.

Browne, A. & Finklehor, D. (1986). Impact of child sexual abuse: a review of the research. Psychological Bulletin, 99 (1), 66-77.

Brunngraber, L.S. (1986). Father-daughter incest: immediate and long-term effects of sexual abuse. Advances in Nursing Science, 8 (4), 15-35.

Cole, C.H. & Barney, E.E. (1987). Safeguards and the therapeutic window: a group treatment strategy for adult incest survivors. American Journal of Orthopsychiatry, 57 (4), 601-609.

Cornell, W.F. & Olio, K.A. (1991). Integrating affect in treatment with adult survivors of physical and sexual abuse. American Journal of Orthopsychiatry, 61 (1), 59-69.

Courtois, C.A. (1988). Healing the incest wound. New York: W.W. Norton & Co.

Courtois, C.A. (1991). The memory retrieval process in incest survivor therapy. Journal of Child Sexual Abuse, 1 (1), 17-36.

Deighton, J. & McPeek, P. (1985). Group treatment: adult victims of childhood sexual abuse. Social Casework: Journal of Contemporary Social Work, 66 (7), 403-410.

Ellenson, G. S. (1986). Disturbances in perception in adult female incest survivors. Social Casework, 67, 149-159.

Evan, G., Kotch, J., & Ringwalt, C. (1988, November). Child abuse and reproductive outcomes. Paper presented at the American Public Health Association 116th Annual Meeting, Boston.

Farraday, A. & Plummer, K. (1979). Doing life histories. Sociological Review, 27 (4), 773-798.

Finkelhor, D. (1984). Child sexual abuse: new theory and research. New York: Free Press.

Finkelhor, D. (1986). A source book on child sexual abuse. Beverly Hills: Sage Publications.

Geiger, S.N.G. (1986). Women's life histories: method and content. Signs: Journal of Women in Culture and Society, 11 (2), 334-351.

Georgas, J., Giakoumaki, E., Georgoulias, N., Koumandakis, E., & Kaskarelis, D. (1984). Psychosocial stress and its relation to obstetrical complications. Psychotherapy & Psychosomatics, 41 (4), 200-206.

Gordy, P.L. (1983). Groupwork that supports adult victims of childhood incest. Social Casework: Journal of Contemporary Social Work, 64, 300-307.

Gorsuch, R.L., & Key, M.K. (1974). Abnormalities of pregnancy as a function of anxiety and life stress. Psychosomatic Medicine, 36, 352-362.

Grossman, F.K., Eichler, L.S., & Winickoff, S.A., (1980). Pregnancy, birth and parenthood. San Francisco: Jossey-Bass.

Harrop-Griffiths, J., Katon, W., Walker, E., Holm, L., Russo, J., & Hickok, L. (1988). The association between chronic pelvic pain, psychiatric diagnoses and childhood sexual abuse. American Journal of Obstetrics and Gynaecology, 71 (4), 589-594.

Hennessy, M.B., & Polk-Walker, G.C. (1990). Case study analysis of pseudocyesis: consideration of the diagnosis of child sexual abuse. Nurse Practitioner, 15 (2), 31-32.

Herman, J. & Schatzow, E. (1987). Recovery and verification of memories of childhood sexual trauma. Psychoanalytic Psychology, 4, 1-14.

Jacobs, J.L. (1991). Child sexual abuse victimization and later sequelae during pregnancy and childbirth. Child Sexual Abuse, 1(1), 111-121.

Jehu, D.(1988). Beyond sexual abuse: therapy with women who were childhood victims. New York: John Wiley & Sons.

Jehu, D., Gazan, M., & Klassen, C. (1985). Common therapeutic targets among women who were sexually abused in childhood. In M. Valentich & J. Gripton (Eds.), Feminist perspectives on social work and human sexuality (pp. 25-45). New York: Haworth Press.

Jones, A.C, (1978). Life change and psychological stress as predictors of pregnancy outcome. Psychosomatic Medicine, 40, 402-412.

Kinsey, A., Pomeroy,W., Martin, C. & Gebhard, P. (1953). Sexual behaviour in the human female. Philadelphia: W.B. Saunders.

Kitzinger, J. (1979). The experience of breastfeeding. Hammondsworth, Middlesex: Penguin.

Kitzinger, J. (1983). Women's experience of sex. Hammondsworth, Middlesex: Penguin.

Knight, C. (1990). Use of support groups with adult female survivors of child sexual abuse. Social Work, 35 (3), 202-206.

Langer, E.J., Taylor, S.E., Fisk, S.T., & Chanowitz, B. (1976). Stigma, staring and discomfort: a novel stimulus hypothesis. Journal of Experimental Social Psychology, 12, 451-463.

Lather, P. A. (1991). Getting smart: feminist research. New York : Routledge.

Lederman, R.P., Lederman, E., Work, B.A., & McCann, D. (1979). Relationship of psychological factors in pregnancy to progress in labor. Nursing Research, 28 (2), 94-97.

Leifer, M. (1980). Psychological effects of motherhood: a study of first pregnancy. New York: Praeger.

Lobel, C.M. (1991). Relationship between childhood sexual abuse and borderline personality disorder in women psychiatric inpatients. Journal of Child Sexual Abuse, 1(1), 71-88.

Lundberg-Love, P.K., Marmion, S., Ford, K., Geffner, R., & Peacock, L. (1991). The long-term consequences of childhood incestuous victimization upon adulthood physiological symptomatology. Journal of Child Sexual Abuse, 1 (1), 89-109.

Maltz, W., & Holman, B. (1987). Incest and sexuality: a guide to understanding and healing. Lexington, Massachusetts: Lexington Books.

McGuire, L.S. & Wagner, N.N. (1978). Sexual dysfunction in women who were molested as children: one response pattern and suggestions for treatment. Journal of Sex and Marital Therapy, 4 (1), 11-15.

McRobbie, A. (1982). The politics of feminist research: between talk, text and action. Feminist Review, 12, 46-57.

Middleton, S. (1988). Researching feminist educational life histories. In S. Middleton (Ed.), Women and education in Aotearoa (pp.127-142). Wellington: Allen & Unwin,

Morrison, J. (1989). Childhood sexual histories of women with somatization disorder. American Journal of Psychiatry, 146 (2), 239-241.

Mrazek, P.J., & Mrazek, D.A. (1981). The effects of child sexual abuse: methodological considerations. In P.B. Mrazek & C.H. Kempe (Eds.), Sexually abused children and their families (pp. 235-245). New York: Pergamon Press.

Mullen, P.E., Romans-Clarkson, S.E., Walton V.A., & Herbison, G.P. (1988). Impact of sexual and physical abuse on women's mental health. The Lancet, 1(8590), 841-845.

Newton, N. (1973). Interrelationships between sexual responsiveness, birth and breastfeeding. In J. Zubin & J. Money (Eds.), Contemporary social behaviour: critical issues in the 70's (pp.77-98). Baltimore: John Hopkins University Press.

Novitz, R. (1982). Feminism. In P. Spoonley (Ed.), New Zealand: Sociological Perspectives (pp.297-305). Palmerston North: Dunmore Press.

Oakley, A. (1979). Becoming a mother. Oxford: Martin Robertson.

Oakley, A. (1981). Interviewing women: a contradiction in terms. In H. Roberts (Ed.), Doing feminist research, London: Routledge & Kegan Paul.

Offerman-Zuckerberg, J. (1980). Psychological and physical warning signals regarding pregnancy: early psychotherapeutic intervention. In B.L. Blum (Ed.), Psychological aspects of pregnancy, birthing and bonding, (pp.151-173). New York: Human Sciences Press.

Omer, H., & Everley, G.S. (1988). Psychological factors in preterm labor: critical review and theoretical synthesis. American Journal of Psychiatry, 145 (12), 1507-1513.

Oppenheimer, R., Howells, K., & Palmer, R.L. (1985). Adverse sexual experience in childhood and clinical eating disorders. Journal of Psychiatric Research, 19, 357-361.

Paddison, P.L., Gise, L.H., Lebovits, A., Strain, J.J., Cirasole, D.M., & Levine, J.P. (1990). Sexual abuse and premenstrual syndrome: comparison between a lower and higher socioeconomic group. Psychosomatics, 31 (3), 265-272.

Pellegrin, E.D. & Thomasma, D.C. (1981). A philosophical basis of medical practice. New York: Oxford University Press.

Peters, S.D. (1988). Child sexual abuse and later psychological problems. In G.E.Wyatt & G. Johnson Powell (Eds.), Lasting effects of child sexual abuse (pp.101-117). London: Sage Publications.

Raphael-Leff, J. (1980). Psychotherapy with pregnant women. In B.L. Blum (Ed.), Psychological aspects of pregnancy, birthing, and bonding (pp.174-206). New York: Human Sciences Press.

Romanik, R.L. (1982). Adaptation to pregnancy due to childhood sexual abuse. Birth Psychology Bulletin, 3 (2), 2-9.

Russell, D.E.H. (1986). The secret trauma: incest in the lives of girls and women. New York: Basic Books.

Schechter, M.D. & Roberge, L. (1976). Sexual exploitation. In R.E. Helfer & C.H. Kempe (Eds.), Child abuse and neglect: The family and the community (pp. 127-142). Cambridge, Massachusetts: Ballinger.

Sheldrick, C. (1991). Adult sequelae of child sexual abuse. British Journal of Psychiatry, 158, 55-62.

Shostak, M. (1989). "What the wind won't take away": the genesis of Nisa - the life and words of a !Kung Woman. In Personal Narratives Group (Ed.), Interpreting women's lives: feminist theory and personal narratives, (pp.228-240). Bloomington: Indiana University Press.

Stanley, L. & Wise, S. (1983). Breaking out: feminist consciousness and feminist research. London: Routledge & Kegan Paul.

Stein, J.A., Golding, J.M., Siegel, J.M., Burnam, M.A., & Sorenson, S.B. (1989). Long-term psychological sequelae of child sexual abuse: the Los Angeles epidemiologic catchment area study. In J. Briere (Ed.),Therapy for adults molested as children: beyond survival, (pp.135-154). New York: Springer.

Summit, R.C. (1983).The child sexual abuse accommodation syndrome. Child Abuse and Neglect, 7, 177-193.

Taylor, S., & Langer, E. (1977). Pregnancy: a social stigma? Sex Roles, 3, 27-35.

Turrini, P. (1980). Psychological crises in normal pregnancy. In B.L. Blum (Ed.). Psychological aspects of pregnancy, birthing and bonding. New York: Human Sciences Press.

Young, I.M. (1984). Pregnant embodiment: subjectivity and alienation. Journal of Medicine and Philosophy, 9, 45-62.

Zuckerberg, J. (1972). An exploration into feminine role conflict and body symptomatology in pregnancy. Unpublished doctoral dissertation, Long Island University, New York.

Other Titles from PCCS Books

The Research Trilogy
AN INCOMPLETE GUIDE TO BASIC RESEARCH METHODS & DATA
COLLECTION FOR COUNSELLORS by Pete Sanders & Damian Liptrot
ISBN 1 898059 02 0

AN INCOMPLETE GUIDE TO INFERENTIAL STATISTICS FOR
COUNSELLORS by Damian Liptrot & Pete Sanders   ISBN 1 898059 03 9

AN INCOMPLETE GUIDE TO QUALITATIVE RESEARCH FOR
COUNSELLORS by Pete Sanders & Damian Liptrot ISBN 1 898059 04 7
This trilogy of books on the subject of counselling research is designed
with the first-time, or timid, researcher in mind. It uses clear language and
counselling examples to guide the new researcher step-by-step through their
research. The books are even fun to read!

AN INCOMPLETE GUIDE TO USING COUNSELLING SKILLS ON
THE TELEPHONE by Pete Sanders   ISBN 1 898059 00 4
The only book on the subject at the time of going to press. Widely used by
telephone helping agencies. Contains several training suggestions for either
groups or individuals.

AN INCOMPLETE GUIDE TO REFERRAL ISSUES FOR
COUNSELLORS   by Steve Williams   ISBN 1 898059 01 2
Steve Williams tackles the problem of how to make, or receive, principled,
satisfactory referrals; how to recognise when you need to make a referral
and why. A useful book for students, trainers and practitioners.

PERSON-CENTRED APPROACHES IN SCHOOLS by Jackie Hill
ISBN 1 898059 07 1
The book teachers have been waiting for to complete their training. This
text contains the blue-print for a way of being in schools that values and
respects the individual, making suggestions for in-house training for staff
and pupils to help tackle the long-standing problems of bullying, poor
motivation, truancy, aggression etc. Even teacher appraisal is included.